DISSOLVING

TOXIC

MASCULINITY

9 Lessons for Raising Boys to Become Empathetic, Compassionate Men

Thomas Haller

M.Div., LMSW, ACSW, CMFSW, DST

Personal Power Press, Inc.

Bay City, Michigan

DISSOLVING

TOXIC MASCULINITY

9 Lessons for Raising Boys to Become

Empathetic, Compassionate Men

© 2018 by Thomas Haller and Personal Power Press

Library of Congress Catalogue Card Number: 2018934278

ISBN: 978-0-9821568-6-5

Printed in the United States of America

Personal Power Press, Inc.
5225 Three Mile Rd., Bay City MI. 48706

Cover Design
Parker Haller, parkerhaller72@gmail.com

Contents

Introduction

A cataclysmic shift in our culture has been brewing for decades. An unimaginable alteration in the fabric of society has finally occurred. We have been thrust into the midst of this change, and we are faced with a serious societal problem. Boys and men have been bombarded with an attitude that has turned masculinity toxic by allowing one set of stereotypical behaviors to define masculinity for all men. Men have learned that to be masculine they must be powerful and unrelenting. Manhood is claimed by taking ownership of things. Money, real estate, social status, and sexual conquest have become the valued commodities that represent power and strength. Power over another, or what sociologists for years have termed "dominance behavior," is seen as the core virtue of masculinity. A set of societal standards now dictates that men be strong, unemotional, aggressive, and dominant over women.

Masculinity in and of itself is not toxic. What made masculinity toxic is the narrowly defined parameters of what it means to be masculine. Most boys are being raised in a system that promotes aggression, power, and rage. They watch their father demand obedience, sit at the head of the table, and be in charge of the family.

They hear his voice turn harsh and gruff when things are not done his way. They are instructed to use violence to solve conflict. They hear the man of the house use phrases like, "Don't start the fight, finish it," "Don't hit first, hit hardest," "Give him a bit of his own medicine," and "Prove you're a man." Boys are often discouraged by their fathers from showing emotion, unless that emotion is anger. They are encouraged to use anger and rage to take charge or to fight back. They witness their father never asking for directions, refusing to seek the advice of others, and being unwilling to go to therapy for help. The underlying message that sons are receiving about women is that men are strong and women are weak, men are superior and women are inferior, men lead and women follow. That message is what makes masculinity toxic.

Sadly, the lessons extend beyond the home. They are taught by sports figures, Hollywood elites, and elected officials who model dominance of women through unwanted sexual advances, sharing of nude selfies, sexual harassment in the workplace, physical assault in the bedroom and in hotel elevators, dismissing a discussion about grabbing a woman's private parts as "locker room talk," distinguishing "legitimate rape" from criminal rape, claiming that how a woman dresses is a determining factor in sexual harassment or rape cases, listening to popular college athletes who are charged with rape calling their victims "career-destroyers," and using the word "rape" in nonsexual contexts: "The wind totally raped my hair," or "My stomach has been raped by the spices in that sandwich."

Decade after decade, we have conditioned our boys to become men who lack empathy and compassion—men who have lost the nurturing side of their beingness. An attitude of dominance has worked its way into our jobs, our schools, our homes, and even our leisure-time activities. For the past thirty years I have worked as a psychotherapist in a private practice, and I have seen the destructive results of a partner who does not admit the effects of infidelity on his relationship; a coworker who blames others for his mistakes; a public official who lacks integrity; a teacher or principal who shames and ridicules students; a father who spanks his children; a college student who seeks a different sexual partner each weekend; a teenage boy who threatens to spread rumors about a girl if she doesn't send him a nude selfie; a husband who repeatedly yells at his depressed wife, "You're a lazy, f**king b**ch. Get off your ass and clean the house"; a father who spends three to four hours every night after work playing video games by himself to unwind from his day; a young adult man who dominates his partner with threats and physical violence; a middle-school boy who demands that his "girlfriend" not talk to any other boys; a high school coach who dismisses his football players' catcalling at the cheerleaders with "Boys will be boys." Toxic masculinity has destroyed marriages, diminished father-son connectedness, impaired father-daughter relationships, sabotaged men's parenting reputation, fractured men's sense of what it means to be a man, and continued the cycle of raising more boys to be toxic masculine men.

It is past time for this narrowly defined view of masculinity to come to an end. It is time to realize that the potential for men to be empathetic and compassionate lies not in bravado and swagger but in our diversity. It is time to celebrate and honor differences and embrace opposing points of view.

Of most importance, it is time to pass on to our children the value of accepting the differences of others and embracing diversity. In our own families we can teach our children how to work together, understand different points of view, and recognize the potential inherent in diversity. We can teach our boys to embrace an attitude of compassion, empathy, kindness, and respect for women. And we don't have to wait for congressional approval to do it. We can begin today without the acceptance or example of our elected leaders. We can succeed at raising our boys to be emotionally healthy masculine men by beginning at home.

Below is a quick glance at the content of each lesson.

Lesson 1: Model the Message

To be an effective teacher of the principles found in the lessons that follow it is crucial that you model the message. How you choose to live your life is the main vehicle in raising boys to become empathetic, compassionate men. This section encourages you to take a look at yourself first. It provides an Effective Role Model Questionnaire you can use to determine your role-modeling quotient. You can also challenge yourself to improve in nine topic areas.

Lesson 2: Teaching a Culture of Accountability

In this lesson you will learn how to teach your son to be accountable for his actions and choices with gentleness and love. By implementing consequences consistently, you allow your son to experience the related, respectful, reality-based consequences that flow naturally from his actions. You will learn how to help your son experience the direct relationship between cause and effect, enable him to view himself as responsible for what shows up in his life, create internal motivation to produce desired behaviors, and develop a healthy masculinity.

Lesson 3: Teaching Self-Responsible Language

A powerful theme runs through Lesson 3: *There is a connection between the words you use, the beliefs you hold, and the actions you take.* In this lesson you will explore the harmful effects of "makes me" language on the development of healthy masculinity. You will learn how to alter your own language patterns and teach boys how to use self-responsible language that takes ownership of their feelings and actions. You will discover ways to help your son develop a language that promotes integrity. Essentially, he will be learning a "foreign" language—the language of responsibility.

Lesson 4: Teaching Suspended Judgment

Lesson 4 will help you create an atmosphere in your home that reflects suspended judgment. You will learn how repetitious judgments categorize and limit what boys see, creating solid beliefs, prejudices, and toxic masculinity. Through the implementation of specific step-by-step strategies, you will expand your son's vision and broaden his perspective, circumvent labeling, and eliminate put-downs, teasing, and name-calling. This lesson will help you teach your son how to end the blame game, let go of the need to be right, and avoid gossip.

Lesson 5: Teaching Empathy and Compassion

Raised with the notion that empathy is the enemy of masculinity, boys learn that expressing sadness, fear, or hurt are seen as weak, soft, and feminine. An increased focus is then placed on the use of anger to express oneself. Lesson 5 introduces you to the empathy deficit that occurs from this narrowing view and shows you how to teach boys to recognize, name, and express their emotions effectively. You learn about tantrum mode and the brain, and how to effectively communicate anger with angry delivery statements. You are given specific directions on how to eradicate the empathy deficit in your home, manage anger, and effectively confront and reduce aggressive behavior. This lesson will guide you in teaching your son to become an assertive *and* respectful, confident *and* compassionate, masculine *and* emotional man.

Lesson 6: Teaching Cooperation, Not Competition

Lesson 6 is your guide to strengthening family unity and helping your son learn the value of cooperation. It presents dozens of specific guidelines for neutralizing the toxicity of competition and developing a sense of oneness and connectedness in your family. In this lesson you will discover a definition of success that will help your son understand what success is and what it is not. You will also learn why you should not run your house like a democracy, how to teach your son that people and feelings are more important than things, the use of rituals and preserving family history, and the importance of making a "Be" choice.

Lesson 7: Teaching Beyond Tolerance

The components that take tolerance to a higher level are the focus of Lesson 7. You will learn how to teach boys to move beyond tolerance to acceptance, then to appreciation, and ultimately to celebration. The Expanding Tolerance steps provided in this lesson will help you to raise boys who recognize and appreciate the differing opinions, beliefs, and practices of those in the family as well as in the community. The diversity in your family and community is embraced, shared, and celebrated. Boys learn that their family is stronger and their community is enriched because of the diversity within it.

Lesson 8: Teaching Sex and Sexuality

Lesson 8 is more than just teaching boys about how babies are made, how to avoid sexually transmitted diseases, and how not to get someone pregnant. In this lesson you learn how to remove obstacles parents face when talking about sexuality, important myths about sex to dispel, topics to confront directly, how to teach boundary setting, and how to talk to boys about rape culture. Through this lesson you will help your son develop the fundamental building block that defines who he is, how he treats himself, and how he treats other people: his sexuality.

Lesson 9: Teaching about Consent

Lesson 9 addresses the topic of consent: what it is and what it is not. Central to this lesson is teaching boys how to ask for consent, give consent, and accept the answer that is given. You will learn the components of consent and the importance of autonomy in giving and receiving consent. Specific steps in the process of acquiring autonomy are provided to guide you in raising a boy who experiences many opportunities and makes responsible choices within them. The instructions in this lesson help you teach boys how to become autonomous while maintaining responsibility, the key to understanding consent.

My partner Valerie and I have taught these lessons in our own home. We have two boys, ages twenty-one and eighteen. Our older son, Reese, is finishing his senior year at a prestigious college in Michigan, majoring in feminism, and is heading off to graduate school in the fall in pursuit of a doctoral degree in feminist epistemology. His younger brother, Parker, is completing his senior year in high school and plans to seek a college degree in aerospace engineering. Both are young adults who are responsible, caring, compassionate masculine men. I am proud for them and who they already are. I am excited for whom they are yet to become and how they will touch the people they encounter along the way.

In the pages you are about to read, I share with you what Valerie and I have done in our home to raise empathetic, compassionate men. Our goal is that you continue our mission of dissolving toxic masculinity in the culture by implementing some of our strategies in your own family.

Lesson 1: Model the Message

Where to Begin

Prior to teaching boys how to become empathetic, compassionate men, it is crucial that you first learn the lessons yourself, practice them in your life, use them with your family, demonstrate them at your work, and incorporate them into the essence of your being. Rid yourself of any toxic attitude toward women that is coursing through your veins. It's important that you start with yourself because attitudes are more easily caught than taught. Children pay more attention to what you do than to what you say. BE the message you want to deliver to your children.

Lesson 1 is for you: *Model the message.*

What if your life IS the message? What if how you choose to live your life is the central learning that enables your son to grow up to be a compassionate man? What if the tips you impart, learning experiences you arrange, lectures you deliver, advice you share, and words of wisdom you speak to your son do not have as much impact on him as the way you live?

Young children need only observe a behavior a few times to be able to reproduce it. They repeat the words they hear. They imitate the actions they see. Adolescents, too, learn by watching and imitating. The mental model you create in their minds and hearts by your behavior is a powerful teaching for children of all ages.

The potential for modeling exists in every moment. You can never turn it off. Telling your children, "I'm not going to model for the next hour, so don't pay attention to what I do," doesn't work. They are still watching, taking it all in, and being influenced by your behaviors.

When your son behaves in a manner that demonstrates toxic masculinity, look at yourself first. Check your attitude. Notice what you're doing. Listen to your tone of voice. Ask yourself, "What role am I playing in my child acting this way?" and "What am I modeling here?" Consider what you could change in your own behavior that would encourage your son to change his behavior.

Be the change you wish to see in your children. Change yourself first and notice how often your child responds appropriately. Use the questionnaire below to help you determine how ready you are to stand in front of your son *as* the message. Read each item and answer Yes or No. See the scale at the end to determine your role-modeling quotient.

Effective Role Modeling Questionnaire

1. _____ I share my feelings with "I" messages.
2. _____ My children see me eat healthy and nutritious foods.
3. _____ I exercise regularly in view of my children.
4. _____ I don't put tobacco, drugs, or alcohol in my system.

5. _____ When I'm stuck and not sure what to do next, my children hear me ask for help.

6. _____ When faced with a crisis, my behavior shows that I am more interested in a search for solutions than in handing out blame and punishment.

7. _____ When I'm feeling hurt or angry, I communicate that with an "I" statement and refrain from sulking, pouting, and yelling.

8. _____ I regularly show affection to my partner in my child's presence.

9. _____ I demonstrate my caring by regularly engaging in activities with my children that they enjoy.

10. _____ I model for my children how to grieve a loss by showing sadness and tears appropriately.

11. _____ I am comfortable in assuming the role of learner on occasion and allowing my child to take the lead.

12. _____ I attempt to create a shared-control style of family management by regularly garnering input from all family members.

13. _____ I model closeness and affection by giving my child regular hugs, smiles, and eye contact.

14. _____ I show by my behavior that *being with* the family is more important than *doing for* the family.

15. _____ I have a support group of close friends whom my children see frequently.

16. _____ My spiritual faith is visible, and I actively engage in it in front of my children.

17. _____ I regularly demonstrate my respect for the environment by refusing to litter, spoil, or waste natural resources.

18. _____ My children know what I value and believe and consistently see me living according to those beliefs and values.

19. _____ My children see me treat living things, including plants and animals, with respect and reverence.

20. _____ I admit to mistakes, and my children see me make amends quickly.

Count the number of times you answered Yes and compare it to the scale below.

20-19 – FANTASTIC – You are regularly demonstrating and modeling what your children need to see from a parent. Give yourself a pat on the back.

18-16 – VERY GOOD – Your children will benefit from your modeling a majority of these values. Congratulations.

15-13 – ADEQUATE – You are showing your children many positive traits, yet you have some work to do. Why not pick out one of the items on the list and begin demonstrating it today?

12 and below – NEEDS IMPROVEMENT – Although you demonstrate some admirable male role-modeling behaviors, you have a lot of work to do. Begin today by adding to your repertoire

of healthy modeling behaviors. Your children and their father are worth it.

EXTRA CREDIT BONUS QUESTION: If you approached each item seriously and answered it honestly, give yourself two bonus points. Now refigure your score.

******

Are there attitudes and behaviors you're proud of? Do you see room for growth in an area in which you would like to improve? Consider the topics below as you review your effectiveness in role modeling.

Love

Every child spells love T-I-M-E. Your presence or lack of presence in your son's life is sending him messages about his importance and about your love. Do you create the time to play catch, shoot baskets, throw water balloons, help with homework, attend the dance recital, play checkers, read bedtime stories, or snuggle on the couch? Are you teaching your son the value of spelling love T-I-M-E?

Crisis

How do you suppose boys learn to deal with a crisis in a nontoxic manner? They learn by watching adults deal with a crisis in a nontoxic manner. Are you teaching that a crisis leads to blame and punishment, or to a search for solutions? When a crisis presents itself in your family, are you teaching your son how to handle it with empathy and compassion?

Communicating Feelings

What type of communication style do you model for your son? When you're angry, do you hold it inside and refuse to talk, giving others "the silent treatment"? Or do you say, "I'm angry. I want to talk about why I'm feeling this way"? Are you prone to yelling and swearing, or to confronting with gentle words? When you're feeling hurt, do you go off alone, stuffing your feelings and refusing to talk about them? Or do you say, "I need some time alone right now. I'll let you know when I'm ready to talk about how I feel."

Seeking Help

When you're stuck and not sure what to do next, do you ask for help? Many boys do not seek help because they don't know how. They don't see Dad stop and ask for directions when he's lost. They don't hear one parent ask the other to help fold the laundry. They don't hear a parent say, "I don't know the answer to that. Let's get some help."

To dissolve notions of toxic masculinity, children need to be introduced to the strategies involved in asking for help—knowing who to ask, choosing appropriate words, locating available resources—by parents who model effective help-seeking behaviors.

Do you regularly ask others for help? Do you ask your daughter or son for help?

Affection

Do you ask your partner to hold hands in view of your son? Do you seek permission from your partner to hug or kiss them in your son's presence? Are you as affectionate with members of the same sex as you are with members of the opposite sex? Does your son see you being affectionate with people whose origins are different from those of your own family? Why not help him see that people are lovable and that affection is about showing care and concern for other human beings regardless of differences?

Disagreement

Do you model how to "fight fair" while resolving an issue? Does your son hear yelling, name-calling, and foul language? Does he hear you blame and shame? Does he see you destroying property to prove your point? Are you teaching him that it takes increased volume to communicate effectively? Or does he observe you listening attentively and making your case in a respectful tone?

Does your son hear you negotiate, ask for clarification, compromise, or agree to disagree? Does he see you apply a solution and evaluate that solution's effectiveness?

Aggression

Do you yell to stop your son from yelling? Do you spank him when he takes a sibling's toy? If so, you are modeling toxic masculinity, the very behavior that you're attempting to eliminate. When you try to stop your son from being aggressive by overpowering him, by taking a position of authority, or by intimidation, you are using a form of aggression to stop aggression, and that is toxic to the development of an empathetic boy.

Aggression is learned. In one research study, 75 percent of aggressive behavior by children ages six to sixteen was in response to a parent's suggestion. The children were simply following the directions of parents who told them, "Stand up for yourself," "Hit her back," "Prove you're a man." Are you teaching your son to use aggression to stop aggression?

Separation and Divorce

When it's time to say goodbye, whether the situation involves divorce, moving across the country, or starting a different job, your behavior speaks volumes to your son.

Many people use anger to separate from others because it makes leaving seem easier and less painful. Becoming angry creates feelings of animosity and resentment, resulting in a gap in the bond with the person being left or doing the leaving.

How are you modeling the separating process? Does your son see you doing it with care and concern? Do you show him how to leave peacefully? Can you model for him how to move to a new situation or relationship with a kind and gentle heart?

Grieving

Do you let your son see your sadness and your tears when you cry? Whether you know it or not, you are modeling for him how to grieve a loss.

As children develop, many things come and go in their lives. This includes toys, clothes, cribs, toddler beds, security blankets, and pets. Perhaps they even lose a grandparent or primary family member. Can you be sad and cry with them? Or do you tell them to "Get over it," or that "Everything will be all right"?

The way you grieve demonstrates for your son how to grieve. Do you want him to isolate himself, become depressed, and harbor resentment or anger? Or do you want him to ask for the space he needs, express sadness, cherish memories, and remain accessible? The choice is yours, and you communicate that choice through your behavior.

<u>Conclusion</u>

Model the message.

Practice, practice, practice. Overdose on practice.

Are you modeling the message you want your son to receive? Practice.

Do you think your son is being disrespectful? Practice.

Are you being the change you want to see in your son? Practice.

Do you see your son struggling with empathy and compassion? Practice.

Are you ready to dissolve toxic masculinity? Practice.

Practice will not make perfect. It will make permanent.

When you practice, you are learning and you are teaching. Practice.

Turn the page and begin. Practice as you go.

Be the model.

Lesson 2: Teaching a Culture of Accountability

Creating a culture of accountability free of toxic masculinity involves developing a desire and a willingness to hold boys accountable for their actions by implementing reasonable, respectful consequences. This nontoxic approach to discipline allows boys to experience both the negative and positive outcomes of their choices and behaviors. Implemented consistently, with gentleness and love, outcomes become the cornerstone of your discipline structure and your son's path to developing responsibility and a healthy masculinity.

Consequences without Severity

Some parents think of a consequence as a form of punishment. They search for a consequence that will be strongly felt, thinking that if it hurts in some way, the child will be sure to retain the lesson. Severity of a consequence sends the message to boys that pain and discomfort are important parts of holding people accountable. They learn that they have to endure pain in order to achieve change in themselves. More concerning, boys learn that they have to create pain in someone else in order to correct them effectively.

The experience of severe discomfort when being disciplined draws the child's focus to the one doling out the punishment—the parent, teacher or coach—and away from themselves and the results of the choices they made. Learning rarely results from severe punishment because children are too busy activating resentment, resistance, and reluctance. They are more likely to spend their time thinking of revenge fantasies and how not to get caught next time rather than about the cause-and-effect relationship between their behavior and the consequences which follow.

It's not the severity of a consequence that holds the impact. Consequences do not have to be severe to be effective. They have to be certain. The certainty that specific, logical consequences follow actions allows boys to learn from the discipline process. Consistency in implementing consequences is the glue that holds a discipline strategy together. Boys learn that if they choose to leave their bike in the middle of the driveway, they are choosing to have the bike hung up in the garage for a few days. Teenagers come to know that if they choose to visit off-limit sites on the computer, they have chosen to lose computer privileges for several days. When the consequence occurs consistently, children can count on it and plan accordingly.

Consequence Is a By-Product of Choice

The point is to help boys understand that a consequence is likely a by-product of an earlier choice. It can be either a positive or a negative outcome. If he chooses to skip lunch, the consequence will most likely be that of hunger later in the day. If your son chooses to leave his clothes on the floor of his bedroom rather than put them in the clothes hamper, the consequence is that the clothes don't get washed, and perhaps he earns the opportunity to do his own laundry from now on. If he chooses to hang his coat on the hook inside the door, the consequence is that he knows where his coat is the next time he heads out into the cold. Choice and outcome are connected.

Cause and Effect Connection

It's important for parents to help their boys make the connection between their current choices and the outcomes those choices produce. Helping boys see the cause-and-effect relationship that exists between the choices they make in their daily lives and the consequences that are directly related to those choices becomes a vital part of your parenting role and a goal of dissolving toxic masculinity.

An effective process for structuring consequences so that boys experience the relationship between cause and effect is to connect responsibilities to opportunities. A child of four is given the opportunity to play with Matchbox cars. He continues to have the opportunity to play with the cars if he chooses to play with them responsibly. If he chooses to throw them after being taught how to play responsibly, he loses the opportunity to play with them. With opportunity comes responsibility. If the responsibility is taken seriously, the opportunity continues. If the responsibility vanishes, so does the opportunity.

In a culture of accountability, opportunities are abundant. So are the responsibilities that accompany those opportunities. When the responsibility is not accepted, then the opportunity is temporarily lost. It sounds like this:

"If you choose not to turn off the video game at the time we agreed upon, then you've decided to lose the opportunity to play video games tomorrow."

"If you decide to come home later than the agreed upon curfew, then you've chosen to lose the opportunity to go out with your friends the next time you ask."

"If you choose to visit computer websites that we've identified as being off-limits, then you've decided to lose access to the computer for [a specified period of time]."

The Dynamic Discipline Equation

The Dynamic Discipline Equation is basic to creating a culture of accountability. In the Dynamic Discipline Equation the consequence is connected to the choice. By structuring the consequences around choices, you help your son experience the cause-and-effect nature of his choices and the results that follow. He learns that opportunity equals responsibility.

A Four-Step Process:

Step 1: Explain the opportunity that your son has and the responsibility that goes with it before you implement any consequences.

"Ozzie, you have the opportunity to play with your brother. Your responsibility is to touch each other gently. If you choose not to do that, you're choosing to lose the opportunity to play with him. You'll be deciding to play in your room for a while."

Step 2: Allow your son to choose the behavior and thus the outcome which follows. This respects his right to choose and gives him a sense of personal power.

Step 3: Follow through immediately after your son's choice either by reducing the opportunity or acknowledging and affirming the responsible behavior. (Give no second chances.)

"Ozzie, remember that in our family opportunity equals responsibility. I see that you're choosing not to touch your brother gently and therefore choosing to lose the opportunity to play with him for now. Looks like you've decided to play in your room for a while."

Step 4: Do give other opportunities to demonstrate responsibility later.

The goal here is to have the boys play gently with each other. This can only be practiced and learned when they're together. Provide as many opportunities as necessary. Reteach how to play responsibly if necessary. Follow through with the consequences as needed. Be consistent.

The Dynamic Discipline Equation becomes the cornerstone of the culture of accountability in your home. The equation is a way to offer boys choices, a degree of control over their own lives, and an opportunity to learn about the relationship between cause and effect.

Compliance Is Not Required

Compliance or noncompliance by the child has nothing to do with the effectiveness of this discipline system. When discipline strategies demand compliance, such as when the parent keeps increasing the severity of the punishment until the child complies, boys learn that adults have power and they don't. Power over another, dominance behavior, is the cornerstone of toxic masculinity. Punishing a boy with increasing severity until he picks up his toys might get him to pick up his toys; however, it also teaches him how to effectively use his power to influence and coerce others to do what he wants them to do. Inadvertently, you have taught your son to keep asking for what he wants from a girl even when she says no. He has learned to increase the severity of his demand or increase the severity of the consequence if his demand isn't met.

In using the "opportunity equals responsibility" discipline strategy, the focus isn't on making the child comply. The goal is to present choices, allows the child to choose, and give him room to learn from the positive or negatives outcomes which occur. With this consequence system boys learn a lesson whether the outcome is positive or negative. It teaches them to take responsibility for their toys or create internal motivation to produce the desired behavior.

Please remember, consequences are not used to control, manipulate, demonstrate power, or get even. Attempting to use consequences for control teaches dominance behavior. Disciplining from the power stance places your son in a position of being "done to" by others in a position of authority. Feeling powerless, he doesn't see himself as being in control of the outcome. He sees himself as the victim.

When boys see themselves as being in control of whether or not they experience consequences or outcomes, they are empowered. They learn to see themselves as the cause of what happens to them. They realize they personally create the results which show up in their lives by the choices they make. This begins to dissolve another aspect of toxic masculinity: the attitude that others are to blame. It's never my fault.

Keep the Consequence Related

When creating a culture of accountability, you need to relate the consequence directly to the behavioral choice made by the child. "If you don't put gas in the car, you choose not to get the car on Friday." "If you drink all the Coke this weekend, you choose to go without Coke the rest of the week." "If you choose to leave your toys out, you have decided to have them placed on the top shelf until Sunday."

If a consequence is unrelated to the behavior, it's interpreted in the child's mind as something you are doing to him. His focus is then likely to be on the person applying the discipline rather than on his choice of behavior. He's not thinking about what he could learn from his choice, or what he could do differently next time. He is focused on the adult and on what is being "done" to him.

While standing on the sideline at a soccer game I overheard a mom talking about her son's upcoming birthday. She was explaining to another parent that she is getting him the cell phone he has been wanting. She stated, "I can hardly wait to give it to him because then I'll have something I can take away whenever he doesn't do what I want." The focus is now on her ability to take a favorite item away rather than on her son's choice to be responsible with the cell phone or not. It is possible that he could choose to lose cell phone privileges but that would only happen if he was misusing the cell phone, not if he didn't do his chores or if he hit his little sister. Keeping an outcome related to a choice is crucial. This may require an adult explaining to the child how specific choices are connected to specific outcomes. In this case, it would be important for the mom to have an in-depth discussion with her son describing what "misuse" means and clarifying what it looks like before she activates the cell phone. This will help him to better understand the connection his choices have to the outcomes that could occur regarding the cell phone use.

Keep the Consequence Reasonable

Another important consideration when creating a culture of accountability in your family is to keep consequences reasonable. Remember, a consequence doesn't have to hurt to be effective. It's not reasonable for your son to be "grounded" from his bike for a month because he failed to put it away one time. It's not reasonable for a young child's toys to be taken away for a week when he doesn't share them with his sibling. It's not reasonable to lose the chance to play your favorite video game for a week because the dishes weren't washed. It's not reasonable to be grounded for two weeks because of a missed curfew. It's not reasonable to lose your cell phone privileges for the rest of a marking period because of low grades.

All of these consequences can be used effectively if applied in a more reasonable manner. Losing the opportunity to ride your bike for three days is reasonable. It also gives your son another opportunity to practice responsibility three days later, while the lesson is still fresh in his mind. Being grounded for the next weekend night, losing toys for two days, and losing cell phone privileges until all missing assignments are turned in are reasonable consequences.

Establishing and implementing a consequence in this way helps boys learn how to make a different choice next time. If the consequence is severe or unexpected, then the learning opportunity is likely to be lost in the boy's feelings of hurt and anger.

__Keep the Consequence Respectful__

In addition to consequences needing to be both related to the behavior and reasonable, they also need to be administered in a respectful manner. When you talk to your son about opportunities, responsibilities, and related consequences, do it with respect and understanding. Set your feelings of anger or disappointment aside. If you implement consequences with a strong tone of anger, your son will tune into your anger rather than into the message you are attempting to deliver. He will learn more about how to talk angrily to produce desired results. Speak calmly, firmly, and seriously to the behavior you want your son to learn to manage.

When implementing consequences, listen as well as speak. Be empathetic as you explain how opportunities were lost. Refrain from using words that attack character or personality. Again, this only teaches your son how to use his words to attack the character or personality of another to intimidate and manipulate. Speak to the situation with a tone that reflects serious concern but not catastrophe.

Respect your son's right to choose, and follow through with reasonable and related consequences applied firmly and consistently. Consequences that are enforced consistently will assist him in learning the relationship between cause and effect. He will see himself as capable of making choices and realize the choices he makes produce results. Consistent consequences will motivate him to make responsible decisions. In time he will learn, "My choices created this; therefore, if I make different choices, I could create something else."

Life Examples

When Brandon Hasleback bought his son Timmy a two-wheel bicycle for his seventh birthday, it did not come without responsibility attached. His father explained the situation this way: "You have opportunities and responsibilities with this bicycle, Timmy. You have the opportunity to ride it in the neighborhood as long as you don't cross Western Avenue. That's too busy a street for bicycle riding. You also have the opportunity to use your bike throughout the day until it gets dark. When it gets dark, your responsibility is to see that your bike is put in the garage. It's important not to leave it outside overnight, where it could easily be stolen. Plus, I don't want to back out of the garage some morning and smash into it. If you take care of your responsibilities, you will keep earning the opportunity to ride your bike. If your level of responsibility drops, so will your level of opportunity."

After asking two clarifying questions, Timmy said he understood.

Three days later, Mr. Hasleback pulled into the driveway after dark and found his son's bike in the middle of his path to the garage. He immediately put the bicycle in the garage. Actually, he did more than put it in the garage. He hung it from ceiling hooks, far out of his son's reach.

At dinner, Timmy was informed that he chose to lose the opportunity to ride his bike for two days because he hadn't taken care of the responsibilities that went with it. "After two days you will have another opportunity to use your bike responsibly," his father explained. "If you choose to handle your responsibilities well, you will continue to have the opportunity to ride."

Timmy knew his father was serious. He also knew he would soon get another opportunity to ride his bike. And he knew his opportunity to continue to ride his new bicycle was under his own control.

*****

Veronica and Tim returned home from their night out to find the babysitter very upset. She told them that their oldest son, Mark, age ten, had spent the evening calling her names and running from room to room hiding. He refused to play with his younger brother and even tried to engage the younger sibling in the name-calling. She described several techniques she used in an attempt to correct the behavior, including time out, loss of television privileges, and no evening snack. Nothing worked.

After hearing about his son's behavior, Tim asked the babysitter, "Can you come back tomorrow for about two hours?"

Hesitantly, she agreed.

That evening, after the babysitter left, Tim and Veronica sat down with their oldest son. Veronica began by explaining, "You had the opportunity to play and watch a video while your father and I went out. We got a babysitter so you and your brother could be safe and have fun playing together. It's not okay for you to call the babysitter hurtful names, and run and hide while she's here. Your responsibility is to play with your brother, listen to what the babysitter says, be safe with your body, and have fun."

Tim continued, "Mark, tomorrow the babysitter will be coming back, and we'll do this a different way. You have lost the opportunity to be at the house while she's here and to play and have fun with your brother. Tomorrow, when the babysitter is here with your brother, you will be with me and your mother while we go grocery shopping."

Mark whined, "I don't like going grocery shopping. It's no fun."

His mother's response was, "You made the decision to join us in grocery shopping by your choice of behavior tonight. Sorry."

When the babysitter arrived the next day, Mark pleaded with his parents to be allowed to stay home. He promised he would behave better and not act the way he had the night before. Even though Mark whined and cried, Veronica and Tim stuck to the plan. Mark accompanied them to the supermarket.

On the way home in the car, Mark asked, "Can I have an opportunity to be with the babysitter and be responsible next time?"

"Yes," Tim and Veronica replied in unison.

Sitting in the car in the driveway, Tim, Veronica, and Mark talked about the responsibilities involved in staying at home when the babysitter was there. Mark agreed to the responsibilities and even suggested a couple himself.

Once inside, Mark asked the babysitter to return the next week so he could have an opportunity to be different when she was watching him and his brother. She agreed.

The following week, Tim and Veronica went out to dinner while the boys had a "movie night" with popcorn and pop. The babysitter reported that both boys chose to use the opportunity to act responsibly.

*****

Esteban watched his adolescent son Raul engage in a fight with another player during a soccer game. The two boys exchanged cuss words and physical blows. Both were ejected from the game and given a two-game suspension according to league rules.

Later that night, Raul complained to his father about how unfair the suspension was. "It wasn't my fault," he said. "He started it. He kept hitting me when the ref wasn't looking. I was just defending myself. I shouldn't have to miss the next two games."

Esteban waited calmly for his son to finish and then said, "Raul, it is never okay to hit others. Regardless of who started it, you stayed involved by cussing and returning the blows."

His son interrupted, "It's just like you to take their side. You never see things my way."

Esteban continued, "I'm not interested in taking a side. What I *am* interested in is you learning from this situation."

"I suppose you're not going to let me play soccer the rest of the season," Raul said.

"Not true," Esteban responded. "By fighting, you have given up the opportunity to play in the next two games, and you can spend that time supporting your team from the sidelines. Tonight you and I are going to talk about how to make a complaint to a ref when you're being mistreated on the soccer field and how to get the coach involved in the process."

The next hour was spent doing just that.

During the next two games Raul sat on the bench and paced the sidelines as Esteban watched the game from the stands as usual. When Raul turned to see if he was still there, Esteban just smiled and nodded his head in approval.

*****

Kevin has two boys, ages seven and eight. They both love to jump. They jump on their beds, on the living room sofa, off the fireplace hearth, from kitchen chair to kitchen chair, down the stairs, over the dog, and up and down in place. They stack chairs on top of each other to make a higher platform from which to jump. Nothing, it seems, is off limits when it comes to jumping.

Since Kevin sees his boys only every other weekend, he doesn't like to impose too many rules. So he lets them jump. He also lets them stay up late, eat whatever they want—mostly junk food—and watch hours of television.

When confronted by his ex-wife about the difficulty she was having getting the boys to do their homework, go to bed at a reasonable time on school nights, and be respectful, Kevin responded, "I don't have any of those problems when they're at my house." "Of course not," the boys' mother replied. "You don't hold them accountable for anything." "Why should I?" was Kevin's retort as he turned and walked away.

What is missing in Kevin's home is a culture of accountability. The lessons his children learn there (We can do whatever we want. If something gets broken, Dad will replace it. Any kind of food is okay for our bodies.) will certainly carry over into other areas of their lives.

Kevin's boys will eventually learn about cause and effect, but the lessons will most likely be embedded in much more difficult life situations.

Conclusion

Teaching a culture of accountability to your son is a simple process. It involves giving him choices and allowing him to experience the positive and negative consequences that flow from those choices. It requires that you follow through consistently and trust the process of designing and implementing consequences.

When you commit to creating a culture of accountability, you trust that your son can learn as much from the consequence as he can from you. You believe that by regularly holding your son accountable he will learn to see himself as the cause of the results he produces. You know that by helping him experience the direct relationship between cause and effect he will create internal motivation to produce the desired behavior, view himself as responsible for what shows up in his life, and develop a healthy masculinity.

Lesson 3: Teaching Self-Responsible Language

One of the most commonly used phrases in our culture is "makes me." For years, we have unknowingly allowed "makes me" and "made me" to invade our language patterns and quietly spread dysfunction throughout our lives and the lives of people our lives touch. The repetitious use of "makes me" and "made me" has contributed to the rise of toxic masculinity. Boys are being raised disowning responsibility for their attitudes and actions and blaming others for their personal negative reactions to events and circumstances. They have become unconscious of the language choices that have programmed them to see something or someone else as being in control of their responses to life.

Unself-Responsible Language

Language which is not self-responsible consists of words and phrases that deny responsibility for one's actions and feelings, blame someone or something else, or keep choices unconscious. Examples include:

"She irritated the heck out of me." (Blames someone else.)

"It wasn't my fault." (Denies responsibility for one's actions.)

"It just came over me. I didn't know what I was doing." (Keeps choices unconscious.)

Toxic masculinity is riddled with unself-responsible language. Although you have heard this kind of language, you perhaps haven't recognized its crippling effect on boys and, ultimately, on developing healthy masculinity.

"Angela makes me happy."

"Don't you make him jealous."

"You're gonna make her cry if you keep that up."

"You turn me on."

"You excite me."

"She turned my head."

"She keeps stringing me along."

"You light my fire."

"She broke my heart."

Harmful Effects of "Makes Me" Language

"Makes me" language leads to a number of unhealthy effects. Physical-level manifestations include anxiety, headaches, hypertension, shallow breathing, high blood pressure, and nervousness. On an emotional level, "makes me" language produces anger, fear, sadness, boredom, depression, worry, unhappiness, dissatisfaction, and frustration. Behaviorally, spouse abuse, tantrums, name-calling, blaming, shaming, drug addiction, excuse-giving, overeating, and smoking can be attributed at least in part to the "makes me" mentality.

Effects of "Makes Me" Language on Boys

"Makes me" is an example of unself-responsible language. Every time boys use that phrase, they strengthen the belief that they are not responsible for their reactions to the people and events in their life.

When that boy becomes a man, he has been programmed to give others both credit and blame for his own emotions. When he says, "Angela makes me happy," he is speaking and thinking in a way that gives Angela credit for his joy. He assigns responsibility for his happiness to her and believes he can be happy only if she behaves toward him in certain ways. His degree of happiness is at the mercy of Angela's behavior.

He uses similar language to blame others for his miseries. "Angela makes me mad." Now Angela is not only in charge of his happiness, she's also in charge of his unhappiness. If she controls both his happiness and his unhappiness, the pressure is then placed on her to do the "right thing" for the man. The "right thing" is defined by the man and could be anything from sending him an iPhone picture of her breasts to cleaning the house and cooking dinner to having sex with him even if she doesn't want to. The man afflicted by toxic masculinity dominates women, and it becomes the woman's responsibility to make him happy in whatever way he expects.

Boys need to be taught that no one can make them feel or do anything. No one can make them mad without their consent. In fact, someone can be actively *trying* to make them mad, and if they don't buy in, the efforts of the other lead nowhere. When boys repeatedly use "makes me" talk, they reinforce the illusion that others can make them feel a feeling or take an action. When they believe that others can make them feel something, their behaviors flow from that belief. They are less likely to take responsibility for their own feelings and actions, assume a victim stance, and blame others for the consequences of their choices.

For boys to grow up to become healthy masculine men, they need to be taught that no one can "turn you on." What really happens is you turn yourself on. You excite yourself by the thoughts you choose to think about another person. If you choose not to think erotic, sexy thoughts about another person, you don't turn yourself on. If you think erotic, sexy thoughts, you excite yourself with them. And the other person doesn't even have to be present for you to do it.

"Makes Me" Variations

"She ruins my day."

No, not correct. How you think about a person's behavior, how you interpret that behavior, the meaning you assign to it, and what you come to believe about it is what ruins your day. You are, in effect, ruining your own day, all the while oblivious to the fact that you are doing it to yourself.

"It's frustrating me."

No, not correct either. *It* doesn't frustrate me. Whatever *it* is, it doesn't have the power to frustrate me. I can only do frustration to myself. I create my own frustration by the thoughts I choose to think and by how I choose to interpret *it*. So do you. The same goes for all of us.

"You're embarrassing me."

No one can embarrass you without your own consent. If you're embarrassed, it's because you bought into the idea that someone else's action reflects on you. When you allow yourself to speak and think in language that reinforces this idea, you give your power to another person. They didn't take it from you. They didn't even need to ask for it. You just gave it to them.

"He let me down."

If he can let me down, then he must be in control of me. My choice of language here reflects a belief that he is in charge of my up/down buttons. When I believe he can let me down or lift me up, I have effectively given him the power to affect my up- or downness. Giving your power away is not a healthy masculine trait.

"He changed my mind."

No, he didn't. You changed your mind after listening to him speak for an hour. It's your mind. Why give him credit for changing something that belongs to you? There is much more personal power in, "I chose to change my mind after listening to his ideas," than there is in, "He changed my mind." Give yourself the credit and the power. After all, it is *your* mind.

"You lost me completely."

Really? You are the one who is lost, but someone else lost you? Own it. Use self-responsible language. "I'm lost. I don't understand. Will you explain that again?" Own the fact that you didn't get it. Ask for help. Responsible behavior is more likely to follow when you choose self-responsible language. Yes, healthy men and boys ask for help.

"He bothers me."

Actually, you bother yourself with the interpretations you attach to what he does. He may, in fact, be consciously attempting to bother you, but if you don't bite the hook he's dangling, you're not bothered.

Self-Responsible Language

Self-responsible language consists of words and phrases that reveal acceptance of responsibility for one's actions and feelings, demonstrate self-ownership of results, or make choices consciously. Examples include:

"I'm creating a lot of irritation about this situation." (Shows responsibility for one's feelings.)

"My response helped create this situation." (Shows ownership of results.)

"I'm choosing to stay away from you right now." (Makes choices consciously.)

Men with healthy masculinity do not use language that attributes their happiness, unhappiness, or any other feeling to an external source. They function under the belief that no one can make them feel anything. It's simply not possible for anyone else to create an emotion in them. Psychologically healthy men know that their emotions are a personal response to an outside act, and it is their responsibility to control them.

Boys raised in homes where language reflects a lack of self-responsibility end up becoming men who speak that language. They consistently choose language patterns that disown responsibility for their behaviors and feelings, deny choice, and portray them as victims. Because that's the language they speak, that's the way they behave. They act irresponsibly, easily assume a victim position, and behave as if they have no choice. Their behavior springs from beliefs that were developed through repetitious use of the language they have consistently heard spoken and now mimic. Healthy men know that no one "makes them" feel or act like a victim.

It is time to make a commitment to teach your son a new language: the language of responsibility. When you teach boys to speak and think self-responsibly, you increase the odds that they will act self-responsibly.

The following strategies will assist you in your quest to establish a family environment where self-responsible language is the norm.

Notice Your Own Language Patterns

Become increasingly aware of your own unself-responsible language. Notice when you make statements like these:

"Don't make me come up there."

"That made her feel bad."

"Stop annoying me."

"Be careful or you'll upset your father."

"Your whining is driving me crazy."

"Don't let me down now."

"You really know how to ruin my good mood."

"You're going to embarrass me."

"You make me want to hug you."

"Sunny days pick me up."

"You are really ticking me off right now."

"You have me all tied up in knots."

Catch yourself and let your children hear you rephrase your statement in self-responsible language. Here is how you might choose to change the phrases above:

"Don't make me come up there" becomes, "I'm coming up there."

"That made her feel bad" becomes, "She felt bad about that."

"Stop annoying me" becomes, "I'm feeling annoyed, please stop."

"Be careful or you'll upset your father" becomes, "Your father may choose to be upset about that."

"Your whining is driving me crazy" becomes, "I'm choosing to be bothered by your whining."

"Don't let me down now" becomes, "I may choose to be disappointed by your actions."

"You really know how to ruin my good mood" becomes, "I changed my mood in response to your behavior."

"You're going to embarrass me" becomes, "I'm planning on choosing embarrassment."

"You make me want to hug you" becomes, "I want to hug you."

"Sunny days pick me up" becomes, "I feel energetic on sunny days."

"You're really ticking me off right now" becomes, "I'm really angry right now."

"You have me all tied up in knots" becomes, "I've decided to feel tied up in knots right now."

A resource you may find helpful in this area is *The Abracadabra Effect: The 13 Verbally Transmitted Diseases and How to Cure Them.*

Do Not Accept "Makes Me" Language

Do not accept language that allows blame to be placed on adults, peers, siblings, or some other external force in your home. Help children learn to restate their "makes me" language.

When your ten-year-old son says, "He made me do it," say to him, "You mean *you chose* to do it. Go ahead and say that. Say, 'I chose to do it.'"

When your teenage son gives you an angry look and says, "You make me so mad," say to him, "You are mad *and* you have the power over that feeling. I don't have power over your feelings. It's okay to just say, 'I'm mad.' You get to be mad at me and still be in control of your feelings."

Rescript "Makes Me" Language

One effective way of rescripting "makes me" language is to change the word that immediately precedes "makes me" to "I." "*You* make me so angry" then becomes, "*I* make me so angry." "That depresses me" becomes, "I'm depressed."

This may sound awkward at first. "I made myself angry," "I make me frustrated," and "I made myself jealous" are certainly not common phrases. Tell your son directly, "This technique puts you in charge of your feelings and actions and helps keep the focus on the real power you have."

Practice it with your son often so he becomes familiar with the sounds of self-responsible speech.

Language That Leaves Boys in Control

Another positive way of speaking that leaves boys clearly in control of their responses is to use the phrase, "I'm choosing." Examples of this technique include:

"I'm choosing to be mad."

"I chose embarrassment when she said that."

"Right now I'm choosing anger."

By encouraging boys to choose such phrases, you are helping them remember the role they play in activating their emotional responses. Bringing their choices to a conscious level increases their options, and they gain a sense of control over their own feelings.

Sunny Day Conversation

We all seem to like the warmth of the sun, playing outside in a cool summer breeze, walking on the beach with the sun shining on our face and a breeze blowing through our hair. Use the opportunity to have a sunny day conversation with your son. Create a discussion about sunshine and its effects on our level of happiness.

Do you think sunshine makes you happy? It's not so. Does sunshine make you happy if you're stranded in a boat in the middle of the lake with no shirt to cover your blistering shoulders? Does sunshine cause happiness if you get new skis for Christmas and are waiting for the season's first snowfall? Does sunshine make you happy if you're a farmer and your crops are parching in the field? No, sunshine doesn't make you happy in those cases. And it doesn't make you unhappy, either.

How you choose to interpret the effect of sunshine and how you choose to think about it is what makes you happy or sad, not the sunshine itself. The sun is not in charge of your happiness.

Language That Promotes Integrity

Using self-responsible language demonstrates integrity. When you behave with integrity, you say what you are going to do and then do what you say. When your actions support your words, other people, including your children, learn that what you say, you mean—that your word can be trusted. Integrity is one sign of a healthy man.

Encourage your son to think through his choices and options, pick one, and state it verbally. Then guide him toward the behavior that reflects the option he chose. When you teach him how to say what he is going to do and how to do what he says, you are teaching integrity.

Boys learn about integrity by watching and listening to the adults around them. When Dad says, "I'll read you that story later," and then doesn't follow through, his child learns that Dad's words can't be trusted. When Mom says, "No, we are not buying a toy at the store today," and then gives in when her son continues to whine, the child witnesses his mother's lack of integrity. When children observe their parents' lack of integrity, they learn that they don't have to match their behavior to their words either.

Conversely, boys learn integrity when they see their parents' behavior aligning with their words. When you say to your son, "We don't use those kinds of words in our house," and those kinds of words are in fact not used, you model integrity. If you say to your son, "The next time you choose to leave your bike in the middle of the driveway you'll lose the opportunity to ride it," and he sees you hanging his bike on a hook in the garage when you find it in the driveway again the next evening, your words have meaning. When you say to your adolescent, "I'll pick you up at five," and you're there at five to pick him up, you demonstrate the use of self-responsible language.

By intentionally selecting words and phrases that demonstrate integrity and encourage self-responsibility, you empower your son and enhance his effectiveness as a capable, caring human being.

Another component of self-responsible language is that of making choice conscious. Use the words "choose" and "decide" to model this concept and help your children become conscious of their choices.

"I'm choosing to get started right away."

"I've decided to save this for later."

"When you choose to throw the trucks, you also choose to play without them for a while."

Practice. Practice. Practice.

Using self-responsible language might sound awkward at first. Many of us are not used to hearing people talk in ways that maintain personal power. Keep on talking. Eventually, it will begin to sound normal.

When your son says things like, "Mom, how come you're talking funny?" or "You sound different, Dad. Why are you talking that way?" know that you are on the right track. Persevere.

When you hear one of your children say, "Mom, I'm okay. I'm just doing irritation right now," pat yourself on the back. Celebrate if your son asks why you're choosing to be in a bad mood. Jump up and down with joy if your teenager corrects your language by saying, "Dad, don't you really mean that you're creating nervousness for yourself right now? You told us nothing has the power to make us nervous."

Bust the power illusions being created in your family by changing your language patterns with the techniques listed above. As you do, you will see those illusions having less influence over the lives of your children. Enjoy the benefits that result from having your entire family living with the reality that each us is responsible for our own feelings. No one can "make us."

Life Examples

During a recent family therapy session, fifteen-year-old Michael started yelling at his parents. "You're so controlling. You tell me everything to do. You won't let me make any decision for myself. You make me so angry." Several times during his venting he repeated, "You make me so angry."

The family therapist stopped Michael at the end of one of his "You make me so angry" statements and asked, "Michael, are you sure you want to give your parents all that power over your feelings?"

"Well, it's their fault I feel this way," Michael snapped.

"Life's easier that way, isn't it?" replied the therapist.

"No, it's not," Michael retorted. "Life sucks around them. They keep me down!"

The therapist looked at Michael and calmly said, "Michael, you're giving your parents power over the one thing you can control: your feelings. It may be true that your parents are controlling and make many decisions for you," he continued, "but you don't have to give them control over your feelings. No one can make you feel a certain way unless you relinquish the control of your feelings to them."

"I'm not sure I get what you mean," Michael said, looking puzzled.

The therapist went on, "What if you started saying to your parents, 'I'm angry when you don't involve me in decisions that affect me.' How do you think they would respond?"

Michael sat quietly for a moment, then said, "I don't know."

"Well, pick one of those things you're angry about and state it to them the way I suggested."

Michael turned to his parents and said, "I'm angry that you made me take Advanced English and never asked me what I thought. I got a D in the class the first marking period and then you guys grounded me because I got such a bad grade."

"You got a bad grade because you refused to work in the class," Michael's father told his son.

"I refused to work because I didn't want to be in that class. None of my friends are in it, and I don't like the teacher."

"Well, we didn't know that," his mother said.

"You didn't know because you don't let me have any say, and then I get angry at you guys."

The therapist quickly interrupted. "Michael, by owning your anger and stating it in a way that accepts responsibility for that anger rather than blaming your parents for it, you've moved the three of you into a solution-seeking mode. Now you can fix the problem together."

The rest of the family therapy session focused on doing just that. Together, with equal input from everyone, Michael and his parents brainstormed possible solutions to the problem. They chose a plan and talked about ways to implement it. Yes, anger was still present in the room, but fixing blame for that anger was not. By owning his anger, Michael *felt* more in control and, as a result, *acted* more in control.

*****

Dominic's parents had been divorced for eight months when he began refusing to plan weekend stays with his father. According to the court ruling, he was to spend every other weekend and one evening during the week at his father's house.

No one knew why Dominic didn't want to go to his father's house. When he was asked about it, all he would say is, "I don't want to go."

Several weeks passed with no change in the situation. Then one evening Dominic's mother, Margaret, overheard a conversation between Dominic and his best friend. "My dad always says that we're going to do something special when I stay at his house, and we never do," Dominic complained. "He says that he'll take me to the movies, and then we sit and watch TV the whole time I'm there. When I ask him about it, he says we'll do something next time, but we don't. There's no use in planning anything with him. He won't do it anyway."

Margaret knew exactly what was happening. Dominic no longer trusted his father's words. He saw that they held little meaning. His mother also knew that if the situation wasn't addressed, Dominic could end up resenting his father and feeling confused about his worth as a son.

With much apprehension, Margaret passed the information on to her ex-husband and told him she expected him to either stop promising to do things or to follow through with his promises. Reluctantly, she threatened to get the court involved if changes were not made at the next visit.

To Margaret's surprise, Dominic returned from his next weekend visit at his father's with a glowing report. He talked about all the things they had done together, none of them involving sitting in front of the television set.

*****

Every weekday morning Roger found himself repeatedly reminding his son Max, "Hurry up and get dressed. You're going to be late for school." Max's predictable response was, "You're making me have to rush." Around and around Roger and Max would go.

"You're going to be late."

"You're making me hurry."

This happened morning after morning until Roger attended a Parent Talk workshop sponsored by Max's school. In the workshop Roger learned about choices and the words to use to place responsibility back on his son's shoulders.

Armed with new verbal skills, Roger vowed to make the next morning different. The next day he walked confidently into his son's room. As usual, he found Max lying on the floor in his pajamas. Roger looked at the youngster and said calmly, "If you choose to go slow in putting your clothes on, it's okay. Just know that you'll be choosing either to go to school in your pajamas or to have to rush at the last minute to get dressed in time. You decide." Then he walked out of the room.

Roger took this same approach every morning. Some mornings Max was dressed and ready to go long before it was time to leave. Other mornings he rushed to get dressed and was putting clothes on as he headed out the door to catch the bus. To Roger's surprise, he never went to school in his pajamas.

Roger stopped arguing with his son and taking the blame for his youngster's feeling hurried. He used self-responsible language to let go of the problem and give the responsibility back to Max.

*****

"I can't mow the grass," Roberto told his father. "It's too hot."

"Nothing is too anything," his father responded matter-of-factly.

"Huh?" Roberto replied.

"Nothing is too anything," his father repeated. "*Too* is a word that people use to prevent taking action and following through. 'It's *too* wet to go outside.' They use it to prevent seeing themselves as able to do something. 'I'm *too* old or *too* young to do that.' They use it to avoid taking responsibility. 'I was *too* mad to think straight.' Some use it to prevent risk or change. 'She's *too* attractive for me to ask out.' How are you using it?" his father asked.

"Dad, it's ninety-five degrees. It's too hot to mow the grass," Roberto insisted.

"Nothing is too anything," his father said once again. "It's possible to mow the grass in ninety-five-degree heat. Stop frequently. Drink lots of water. Take long breaks."

"Okay, it is possible," Roberto conceded, "but I don't want to do it right now."

"Then you choose not to?" his father asked.

"That's right," said Roberto. "I choose not to right now."

"Thanks for hanging in there with me on this, Roberto," his father said. "Saying you choose not to mow right now sounds a lot more self-responsible that saying it's too hot. I appreciate your using language that makes your choice conscious."

"Oh, Dad!" Roberto responded with a grin, revealing both his admiration for his father and his frustration with the situation.

*****

Carl watched his son Marcos step out of the car in full soccer gear and place his soccer ball next to the back steps as he took off his shoes before entering the house. The routine was to place all his soccer gear in the sports bag and have it ready for the next practice. Marcos followed through with the routine in usual fashion, except for the soccer ball, which was left next to the steps.

Two days later, when Marcos was getting ready for soccer practice, the ball was not in his bag. Furious, he turned to his younger brother and began accusing him of taking his ball without permission and not putting it back.

Carl, remembering where the ball had been placed, stepped in to help his younger son, who had no clue why he was being verbally attacked by his brother. "It's not okay to talk to your brother like that," Carl said to Marcos. You are responsible for your own soccer equipment. Your brother had nothing to do with your ball."

"He must have," Marcos shouted.

"That's not true," Carl told him. "Take responsibility for your own actions by retracing your steps the other night when you came home from practice, and I think you'll figure out what happened to your soccer ball."

With much grumbling, Marcos grabbed his soccer bag and headed out the door. A few minutes later he returned with his head hanging down and a soccer ball in his hands. He had found it next to the steps, exactly where he had left it.

Carl looked at Marcos and said, "I think you need to say something to your brother before we leave."

Marcos walked over to his younger brother and quietly said, "I was wrong in accusing you of doing something with my ball. Next time I'll be gentler with my words, and maybe I'll ask you for some help."

Carl put his arm around Marcos and gave him a hug. "Let's go to soccer practice," he said, and off they went.

Conclusion

There is a powerful theme running through this lesson. Put simply: *There is a connection between the words you use, the beliefs you hold, and the actions you take.* Yes, your language patterns influence your behaviors.

"Actions speak louder than words," you may be thinking. Or "Be a doer, not a talker." Or, as one workshop participant recently told me, "Words are cheap."

Words are not cheap. They are the most valuable currency you possess if creating a self-responsible boy is one of your parenting goals. The words your son uses create his thoughts. His repetitious thoughts become his beliefs. And his beliefs influence his actions. If you want to raise a boy to become a man who demonstrates self-responsible behaviors, begin by teaching him self-responsible language.

Lesson 4: Teaching Suspended Judgment

The Judgment Trap

The judgment trap begins with our rush to evaluate. We compare, rate, score, judge, and assign value to movies, meat, eggs, music, furniture, cars, people, animals, left-handed pitchers, horses, and members of the opposite sex. We rank television programs, tennis players, and lovers. We identify the world's best-dressed men, determine the top twenty college basketball teams, and choose a Miss Universe. We evaluate our jobs, our coworkers, and ourselves. Nothing, it seems, escapes the critical, judgmental, evaluative mindset of our culture. Judging others as good or bad, right or wrong, skinny or fat, smart or dumb is toxic to our society and to the development of boys.

There seems to be no escaping judging or being judged. It's everywhere in our culture. It begins at birth. Within minutes of your son's appearance on earth he was being judged as healthy, cute, strong, homely, loud, or fussy. People may have remarked, "He's such a happy baby." As a toddler, the judgment continued. He was constantly being evaluated: when he walked and talked, how long he took naps, how often he whined or smiled, and where and when he went potty.

Then he went off to school and the judgment intensified. There your son was tested and rated on his level of mastery on a narrow skill set that has little to do with real learning. He was given external judgmental measures of his effort, including stars, stickers, smiley or frowny faces, student-of-the-week awards, public performance charts, and grades. Parent/teacher conferences were held and he was compared to other students, using grade-level norms.

You and your son now live in a society that is obsessed with ranking, scoring, comparing, and attaching ratings to movies, sports teams, meat, cars, music, stocks, and more. People are judged as being lazy or ambitious, boring or stimulating, ugly or beautiful, stupid or intelligent, weak or strong. Nothing, it seems, escapes the critical compare-and-contrast mindset bred into our culture.

The Limits of Judgment

Judgment limits how we see people. When we judge another person as uncaring and use language that reflects that view, we reinforce a belief that the person is uncaring. A series of mental processes begins which is designed to prove us correct. The mind becomes programmed to notice uncaring rather than caring acts. Over time, this selective noticing creates a biased interpretation and a narrow view of the person in our mind. They become the label we have assigned to them rather than a fully functioning human being who possesses and manifests a wide range of behaviors and attitudes.

Judgment keeps us from seeing clearly. If we judge someone as old, we're not as likely to see behavior that reflects youth. If we judge someone as ugly, we're not as likely to notice their beauty. If we judge someone as gifted, we tend to become preoccupied with their giftedness and miss the characteristics they have in common with others.

Judgment has wreaked havoc on masculinity. It has narrowed boys' and men's vision and solidified perspective. Boys grow up spending their time determining if people, places, or things meet their mental model of how the world should be instead of accepting it as it is. Their judgment categorizes and limits how and what they see. As boys transition to manhood, they create a narrow and distorted picture of the people around them. Over time, the repetitious judgments turn into solid beliefs and prejudices.

How can parents, teachers, coaches or anyone coming in contact with boys on a regular basis help them get out of the judgment trap? How can adults decrease the likelihood that boys will be snared in judgment and confined by it?

Start early, and regularly practice the following behaviors in your family.

Drop Labels from Your Vocabulary

When you label someone, you are judging them and making an evaluation of their worth based on incomplete information. Labeling another person as dumb, dishonest, boring, or unhelpful narrows your view of them in your mind. By using a one-word description, you take all their characteristics, abilities, attitudes, and personality traits and squeeze them into one concept. You then tend to see that person as the label you have put on them.

No characteristic, no ability, no personality trait or attitude exists in pure form. All of us are a mixture. We are part honest and part dishonest, part intelligent and part not so intelligent. We are both helpful and unhelpful, coordinated and uncoordinated, at varying times. So are our boys.

All labels, negative or positive, are confining. They categorize and pigeonhole. Being seen as athletic is as limiting as being seen as nonathletic. Labeling a boy athletic draws attention to his athletic skill and sends the message that it's a desirable trait for a boy. While it's okay to *be* athletic, being labeled that way ignores skills and interests that are not athletic, such as photography or cooking. Boys who demonstrate abilities or interests in such nontraditional areas risk being seen and labeled as not masculine, perpetuating a narrow definition of masculinity that leads to toxicity.

Teach boys to replace labeling with description. When you hear your son labeling a peer, direct him to use words that describe what he sees going on. "She's a cheater" is a label. "She added her score incorrectly" is a description. "He's a liar" is a label. "He withheld important information" is a description. "He's a klutz" can be restated as, "He was uncoordinated with that move." "She's a slow learner" can become, "It took her a week to understand how to divide fractions." "He's a loser" can be stated as, "He struggles to understand chemistry." "She's lazy" can be rephrased as, "She waited until the last minute to do her homework."

Replace Judgment with Description

People also place judgment on things, not just on other people. Use every opportunity to teach your son how to suspend judgment by replacing his judgmental statements about the world in which he lives and interacts with descriptions.

If you hear, "The weather is crappy," restate it as a description. "It's ten degrees with a wind chill of minus thirteen."

If your son says, "The car is a piece of junk," rephrase the statement. "There is rust around all the fenders, little tread on the tires, and the air conditioner doesn't work."

"This math is stupid" can be stated as, "The math we're learning right now is difficult for me to understand."

"The cell phone service sucks" can be described as, "I'm only able to get one bar of WiFi strength right now."

When boys learn to describe their experiences rather than judge them, they learn the skill of reducing judgment in whatever situations they encounter in life.

Avoid Being Right

One payoff we get from judging is that of being right. Being right is a reward that helps to perpetuate our evaluative thinking. It's a way of proving our worth to ourselves and others. However, being right comes with a price. It alienates us from others. When we set ourselves up to be right while judging others to be wrong, we concentrate on differences rather than on commonalities. In the process, we promote a "me vs. them" mentality. When boys start to think this way, they take a huge step toward toxic masculinity.

Raise your sons to understand there can be more than one right way of doing things. Help them see that others may have a different perspective or belief, and it doesn't make them wrong. When a boy grows up in an environment where he sees there are always more options, ideas, concepts, theories, or solutions available in a diverse family and community, he learns that being right doesn't work.

Use language that reflects openness to differing perspectives:

"That's another way to think about it."

"I hadn't considered that approach."

"You always have more options than you think you have."

"Who could you ask for a different perspective?"

"If you were to switch places with your sister, what might the situation look like then?"

"Let's explore your idea further and see how it turns out."

"Your answer is one possibility."

Eliminate Put-Downs, Teasing, and Name-Calling

Name-calling or put-downs are judgmental. Put-downs are intended to drop the other person to a level below you.

"Nice going, stupid."

"What a klutz."

"She's a barker."

Put-downs with a sarcastic flavor are very popular with kids, who often attempt to hide the judgment with a hint of humor.

"If she had half a brain, she'd be dangerous."

"I don't see how he can walk and chew gum at the same time."

"He'd forget his head if it wasn't attached."

When you allow put-downs to occur in your family, even when they seem harmless, you are teaching your boys how to pass judgment and cover it with humor. They move further down the continuum toward toxic masculinity.

Teasing is never appropriate in loving families. Humorous teasing or making fun of someone is having a laugh at someone else's expense. No matter how insignificant it seems to be, it still hurts. When boys are on the receiving end of teasing, they find themselves in a defensive position and often feel they have to attack back to create balance and save face. They learn how to establish dominance by keeping others down with words. They practice in the family while they're growing up, and in adulthood using words as a weapon becomes commonplace when talking to their spouse or coworker.

Dismissing teasing as "I was just kidding" undermines the lesson of suspending judgment. What is said in supposed jest is simply a veiled attempt to put another person down. Although the judging statement may contain a bit of truth recognized by both the sender and the receiver, both the one doing the judging and the one receiving it are harmed in the process. The judger is harmed because he perpetuates the judgmental mindset that keeps him stuck in distorted beliefs and prejudices. The one being judged is harmed because the subconscious mind doesn't take it as a joke. The subconscious mind simply records what is spoken or thought. It doesn't differentiate between put-downs that were meant as jokes and those that weren't. The impression of being judged is recorded regardless of its intention, and toxicity grows.

Confront your son whenever you hear him use a put-down, teasing, or name-calling. The discipline strategy outlined below is called the One-Minute Behavior Modifier. It can be used to put an end to any unwanted behavior. An in-depth explanation of this strategy can be found in *The Only Three Discipline Strategies You Will Ever Need.* Follow the three steps in putting an end to put-downs, teasing, and name-calling in your family:

Step One: Name the child and the behavior.

"Michael, that's name-calling."

Step Two: State the reason for elimination.

"We don't name-call in this family because it hurts feelings and creates a disconnect between family members."

Step Three: Teach a new behavior.

"When you're angry at your sister, you can say, 'I'm angry. I don't like it when you don't let me have a turn.'"

Putting it all together, it sounds like this:

"Michael, that's-name calling. We don't name-call in this family because it hurts feelings and creates a disconnect between family members. When you're angry at your sister, you can say, 'I'm angry. I don't like it when you don't let me have a turn.'"

Or

Step One: Name the child and the behavior.

"Antonio, that's a put-down."

Step Two: State the reason for elimination.

"We don't use put-downs in this family because it creates divisiveness and generates angry feelings."

Step Three: Teach a new behavior.

"What we do here is tell the other person how we're feeling and what we would like to have happen."

Putting it all together sounds like this:

"Antonio, that's a put-down. We don't use put-downs in this family because it creates divisiveness and generates angry feelings. What we do here is tell the other person how we're feeling and what we would like to have happen."

Stay Away from Gossip

Most gossip is pure judgment based on insufficient information. It is full of put-downs, rumors, interpretations, and judgments. It is divisive, separating, and nonproductive. Gossip is riddled with misinformation, limited perspective, and criticism. It is used to manipulate how one person thinks about another person. It creates an atmosphere of *better than*. We are better than them, men are better than women, my way is better than her way, whites are better than blacks. There is no such thing as constructive gossip.

Do not allow gossip in your home. When you hear it, step in immediately and say, "That sounds like gossip. Talking about other people when they're not here to offer their perspective is hurtful and can be damaging to their reputation. Let's change the subject and talk about something else."

Teach your boys to walk away from gossip and to never engage in it.

Refuse to Play the Blame Game

Focus your parenting on fixing the situation rather than on fixing blame. Find a solution instead of finding fault. Blame and faultfinding serve no useful purpose in raising boys to become empathetic, compassionate men. Energy spent blaming your son for forgetting to feed the dog doesn't insure that the dog will be fed tomorrow. Finding fault with your teen's decision to come home late does nothing to move him toward finding a workable solution. Blame and faultfinding teach your son to deny, disown, and discount problems, sweep them under the rug, pretend they don't exist, and push the problem onto someone else.

Men infused with toxic masculinity see women as the problem when they are accused of sexual harassment. They believe and subsequently remark, "If women wouldn't dress so provocatively, they wouldn't get approached by men." The focus is shifted away from men and their behavior and placed on the way a woman dresses, looks, walks, talks, sits, how much alcohol she's been drinking, or just about anything else. The real problem is that boys have been taught to blame something or someone else, rather than look inside and take responsibility for their own choices and behavior.

To raise a boy who is not infused with the blame game, teach your son a self-examination process. Instead of blaming others and training his mind to find fault elsewhere, help him use his time and energy understanding how his perspective has influenced his responses and examining his role in the situation at hand.

Teach him the DANAP Strategy: Describe - Ask - Next Time - Action - Practice

Step One: Describe the situation. Act as if you are a reporter for the local TV station. Be factual and honest as you use descriptive words to paint a picture of what has taken place.

Step Two: Ask yourself these two questions. Answer openly and honestly.

"What role did I play in this drama?" and "What did I do to help perpetuate this situation?"

Step Three: Explore Next Time behaviors. What could you do differently next time that would alter the outcome? Brainstorm possible changes in the words you used this time, alterations in the thoughts you had about the situation, adjustments in beliefs you've held and assumptions you've made, and changes in behavioral choices that would result in a different outcome next time.

Step Four: Create an Action plan. What is one thing (or maybe two) from your above list that you will change within yourself or actively do to: (1) prevent the situation from occurring? or (2) in the event that it does occur, act differently to alter your role in the outcome?

Step Five: Practice the plan. Act as if the new behavior is true of you until it is true in fact. Practice using different words or having different thoughts until they become part of who you are.

Life Examples

Bob was fishing with his teenage son Tom in the early evening. As the sun was setting and twilight spread over the lake, the fish began biting regularly. Before they realized it, darkness had settled in, and it was time for the father/son duo to head to shore.

Bob was reeling in the last line when he heard an unfamiliar voice. In the fishing frenzy, Bob had forgotten to turn on the boat lights, and a DNR officer had pulled alongside their boat to discuss the matter. After briefly talking over the issue, the officer handed Bob a one-hundred-dollar fine that covered several minor boating infractions he had observed.

On shore, while packing up the fishing gear, Tom found a large, expensive flashlight. "Look," he told his dad excitedly, "the DNR guy left us a little gift. I guess that's what he gets for being such an ass and writing us that ticket." Bob didn't say a word.

When the truck was packed, Bob and Tom jumped in the front seat, but instead of taking the route home, Bob surprised his son by heading to the other side of the lake and the local DNR office, a destination twenty miles out of their way.

When they arrived at the office, Bob went inside and asked to speak to the officer whose name was on the bottom of the ticket. Tom figured his dad was going to give the guy an earful. When the officer appeared, he too figured he was in for an earful.

Instead, Tom and the officer both learned a valuable lesson.

"Did you lose a flashlight this evening?" Bob asked the officer. "Yes," the officer replied, looking somewhat stunned.

"I have it. I'll be right back," Bob told him. A moment later, he returned with the flashlight in hand and gave it to the officer. Still stunned, all the officer could do was offer a simple, "Thank you."

On the drive home, Tom inquired about his dad's behavior. "How come you returned the flashlight after how that jerk treated you?"

Bob smiled and said, "We don't need to blame the man for simply doing his job. We had several boating infractions. If we didn't have those infractions, there would have been no reason for the ticket. Our lack of responsibility had nothing to do with the flashlight, and it wasn't our flashlight to keep."

******

Can you imagine parents giving their children formal gossip lessons? Can you envision them teaching their children the specific skills necessary to become proficient at the art of gossiping? That is exactly what David and Samantha Welder do when they talk about other people in front of their children. Through the evening gossip sessions that include talking about friends, relatives, and other children, David and Samantha are training their own children to duplicate their values, behaviors, attitude, and style of language.

*****

Samantha walked in the door from work to find her son waiting in the living room.

Carl wasted no time in saying, "Mom, we need to talk."

There was a moment of silence as Samantha sat down. "What happened?" she asked.

"Well, I'm not sure, but I think my girlfriend is pregnant."

Samantha stood up immediately. "What? You think she's pregnant? You had sex with that girl, Carl? You're fifteen. What were you thinking? I can't believe you would do this to yourself, to her, and to us. How long have you been having sex with her? Oh, I don't want to know! I just can't believe you could be so stupid, after all we've taught you."

Carl's mother threw up her hands and walked out of the room. Unsure of what to do next, and with tears running down his face, Carl walked out the back door.

Later that evening, Samantha and her husband spent several hours frantically searching for their son. After calling all his friends and the police station, they received a phone call from Carl's wrestling coach, who had returned home from a late dinner out with his wife to find Carl sitting on his front porch. After talking with his coach for close to an hour, Carl finally decided to call home and see if his parents were ready to listen to him.

Samantha missed a chance to join her son in the initial stages of this learning opportunity. Later, she was able to stop fixing blame and start addressing the problem. Sadly, because of her judgmental attitude, her relationship with her son was never the same as it was prior to the incident where he had shared his news about his girlfriend's pregnancy. At the age of twenty-five and with a college degree behind him, Carl still hesitates to share personal information with his mother. He fears being judged.

*****

Roberto and Arianna are adolescent siblings, one year apart in age. Roberto is the oldest and also the biggest. He stands six inches taller and weighs forty pounds more than his sister. He uses his height, weight, and age difference to his advantage whenever he wants to exercise power at the expense of his younger sibling.

When Roberto wants his own way, he stands up, towers over his sister, waves his finger in front of her face, and occasionally pokes her. His parents have sent him to his room, yelled at him, ridiculed him, and put their fingers in his face. Not surprisingly, none of those maneuvers worked to eliminate the behavior on a long-term basis.

After attending one of my parent trainings, they switched tactics. They decided to use the One Minute Behavior Modifier.

"Roberto, that's intimidation," his father told his bullying son when he next saw the behavior. "It's not appropriate in our family because it creates fear in the person being intimidated. Fear is not a motivator in our home. What we do here is use language to try to convince the other person to do things our way. If that doesn't work, we accept their decision, sometimes reluctantly."

Roberto's parents had to use their verbal statement on several occasions before their son figured out they were serious about creating a family environment free of fear-based tactics. Over time, he learned to speak up for himself skillfully while at the same time showing respect for the opinion of his sister. He was able to move away from toxic masculinity and closer to healthy masculinity.

*****

Fred and Paul are brothers, three years apart in age. Nine-year-old Fred is the oldest. The brothers have pedal carts they operate up and down the long driveway that leads from the road to their house and horse ranch.

Fred, being older, can go faster and make more intricate maneuvers with his pedal cart than his younger brother can. Fred gets a lot of enjoyment from bumping his brother's cart and cutting him off by pulling in front of him. Paul gets frustrated, and Fred enjoys that even more.

In an effort to control sibling rivalry and teach the values that are important to her family, Fred and Paul's mother implemented the One Minute Behavior Modifier. "Fred, that's cutting your brother off," she said when she observed the behavior. "That's not helpful because it slows him down. He can't pedal as well when you cut him off. That makes it no fun for him. What would be helpful is for you to keep going fast so you can both have fun."

*****

Ray is a teenage boy who visits his father on alternate weekends. The father is more lax than his former spouse when it comes to discipline issues. He appears to have only a few, poorly enforced, rules of behavior at his home.

Reentry into the mother's home after a weekend with the father is creating problems for Ray and his mother. Ray resents the restrictions at his mother's and comes back angry. His anger often takes the form of cussing.

"Ray, that's cussing," his mother tells him. "Cussing isn't permitted here because cuss words have a vulgar ring and aren't respectful of me as a woman and as your mother. Also, they're not necessary to get my attention. The way to get me to listen to your concerns is to use non-cussing words. When you're really angry, you can write down your thoughts and feelings any way you want and go back and cross out the cuss words. If you do that, I will read what you wrote thoroughly and respond." And once again a behavior is transformed by a parent who believes young men should use respectful language even when they are angry.

*****

Fourteen-year-old Eric was a master at delivering vicious put-downs to other family members. "That's stupid," he would tell his sister. "You're dumber than rocks," he once told his younger brother, reducing him to tears. These are a few of his favorite expressions:

"You're an idiot."

"You're sneakier than snake oil."

"You are one ugly duck."

"Ask me if I care."

"You call that intelligent?"

"I think your sense of humor just flew out the window."

In an effort to heal the divisiveness in his family, protect his other children, and help Eric learn a kinder, more appropriate and nontoxic behavior, his father turned to the One Minute Behavior Modifier. He knew that his son's verbal insults were different than teasing. His comments were verbal violence that sometimes led to physical violence in his family. So "verbal violence" is the name of the behavior he chose to use with his family.

"Eric, that's verbal violence," this concerned father stated when he heard his son call his sister retarded. "We don't use verbal violence in this family because it puts other people down and destroys connectedness and trust. If you're angry or frustrated with your sister, tell her how you're feeling and what you would like to have happen. This is what it might sound like. 'Sherry, I get really frustrated when you giggle so much. I'd like it if you could keep that under control at the dinner table.'"

Eric thought his dad's request was stupid so the verbal violence continued. So did use of the One Minute Behavior Modifier. Eric's father used the technique in a variety of situations over several months. The behavior did improve significantly.

<u>Conclusion</u>

Does the atmosphere in your home reflect suspended judgment? Do you expand your son's vision and broaden his perspective by eliminating words of judgment? Do you label your children as spoiled, lazy, rude, obnoxious, or as outgoing, athletic, motivated, kind, polite? Positive or negative, a label is a label.

Judgments categorize and limit how and what boys see. Repetitious judgments turn into solid beliefs, prejudices, and toxic masculinity. Teaching your son how to use description instead of labeling; eliminate put-downs, teasing, and name-calling; end the blame game; let go of the need to be right; and avoid gossip will provide him the best opportunity to grow into a man of compassion, empathy, and confidence.

Lesson 5: Teaching Empathy and Compassion

To become empathetic, compassionate men, boys need adults to clarify and interpret the world around them. Without helping young boys personalize and make sense out of values through debriefing and direct teaching, we leave them to make emotional and cognitive sense of the world on their own. This is a difficult task for many boys. Often, they don't know what feelings they are experiencing or what to do with them. In an attempt to manage their thoughts and feelings, they act them out, many times in ways that adults interpret as "bad behavior." Without guidance from teachers, coaches, and parents in what to do and how to respond to their world, boys will guide themselves by repeatedly making the same choice or by randomly making a different choice, with little or no conscious connection to internal feelings and processes.

Developing Emotional Intelligence

Helping boys develop a high level of emotional intelligence is crucial to the health of their masculinity. One mark of toxic masculinity is the increased focus on the use of anger to express oneself. Expressing sadness, fear, or hurt is seen as weak, soft, and feminine. Boys are ridiculed and chastised for crying, being scared, and expressing pain. They live in a culture in which they are exposed to models of empathy deficit. They grow up hearing statements such as:

"Stop crying."

"Don't worry about it. You can get another one."

"It's not that big a deal."

"So what do you want me to do about it?"

"Why don't you just suck it up?"

"Pouting isn't going to get you anywhere."

"Man-up and get back out there."

"Stop being such a wuss."

"You throw like a girl."

"You're so pussy-whipped."

"You're too sensitive. Don't let it bother you."

"You shouldn't be scared."

"Boys don't cry."

"Come on. Get over it."

"You're overreacting."

"If you don't stop crying I'll give you something to cry about."

A Chronic Condition

Empathy deficit is a chronic condition brought on by adults' refusal to acknowledge a boy's feelings or by their efforts to diminish those feelings when they are expressed. These symptoms stem from adults who believe that to be a man means one has to be strong in the face of adversity, aggressive when confronted, never show emotion, and take control of the situation. Having an empathetic response to a situation is seen as a sign of weakness and should be avoided.

Raised to believe that empathy is the enemy of masculinity, boys don't learn how to recognize, name, and express their emotions effectively. They learn to use the one emotion they are permitted to express, anger, as a way to communicate sadness and hurt. When they're feeling hurt, they get mad at the person they identify as having caused the hurt. When they're sad, they express anger at the event or person they perceive as having caused the sadness. Angry boys become angry men, who in turn use aggressive behavior to control the situation or person with whom they are angry.

A Lack of Closeness

Long-term existence of empathy deficit results in a lack of closeness between men and their partners, children, and coworkers. Lack of empathy produces a severe disconnect that can take years to repair. Women are often left bewildered at men's apparent lack of caring and concern for their feelings. Children learn to numb their feelings as a coping mechanism to protect them from experiencing the hurt and emptiness they feel in response to their father's emotional distance.

Because many men have a low emotional quotient, they don't realize their homes have been infected by an empathy deficit. Not being consciously aware of the problem, they allow the condition to exist and get progressively worse as their boys grow older, leading to the epidemic of toxic masculinity from which our culture is suffering.

Reversing Empathy Deficit

The empathy deficit can and must be reversed in our homes and in our boys' daily lives. When a deficiency is present, whether in the home or school, education plus action is the pathway to health.

Use Feeling Words

To eradicate the empathy deficit in your home, begin by understanding its importance. To be fully healthy, boys need parents, teachers, and other adults to respond to their feelings in positive ways. This includes using feeling words when boys are caught up in strong emotion (sadness or joy, anger or love, fear or faith).

"You look like you're frustrated."

"You seem angry."

"You sound like you're bubbling over with happiness."

"You seem disappointed in the grade you received on the last math test."

"You sound like you're hurting inside at the way your girlfriend treated you."

"You sound excited."

Statements that acknowledge a range of feeling states communicate to boys that their feelings are normal and part of being a fully functioning human being. Such acknowledgment serves as an inoculation against empathy deficit.

Lead with Empathy

Lead with empathy when combating this debilitating deficit. Teaching, reassuring, disciplining, explaining, and providing information can come later. When your son is in the midst of powerful emotion, telling him there is no good reason for his feelings exacerbates the problem inherent in toxic masculinity.

"I see tears in your eyes. You look sad" leads with empathy. So does, "So you felt envious when you saw his new bike."

Demonstrate understanding by telling your son, "You took the loss hard. Do you want to talk or be left alone for a while?" Show him that empathy deficit has no place in your home by saying, "You're really concerned about that," and "It's okay to feel bad for a while."

Establish Proximity

Giving love, nurturing, and comfort through physical touch or closeness when boys are upset puts empathy deficit on the run. Lift your son onto your lap and hug him if he fell and skinned his knee. Hold your five-year-old if he's scared of the shadows in his bedroom. Rub your son's back if he's crying so hard he can't seem to get his breath. Sit quietly next to your teenage son who just broke up with his girlfriend.

When your son is experiencing emotion, establish proximity. In our society we tend to be either physically close and emotionally closed, or physically distant and emotionally open. Simply be in his vicinity more often than you normally would. You don't have to DO anything. You don't have to SAY anything. You just have to BE there. This sends a powerful message that being emotional is accepted here. You are letting your son know that he can be physically close AND emotionally open.

Acknowledge Feelings

Acknowledge a boy's feelings even if you have to guess what he might be feeling at this moment. Attempting to talk a boy out of his feelings perpetuates the notion that they are invalid and he shouldn't be having them. "You seem frightened" teaches empathy. "There's no reason to feel scared" is empathy deficit in action. "It must feel bad not to get invited to the party" communicates understanding and caring. "There will be other parties. We can have one of our own" tells the boy that his feelings are not important.

Create Venting Time

There are times when boys send nonverbal signals indicating some degree of distress. You may see a clenched fist, furrowed eyebrows, crossed arms, a frowny face, or a defiant glare. These and other clues signal that emotions are brewing. At times it's helpful to give boys who bury their hurt, ignore their sadness, or seethe with anger an opportunity to vent.

Use language that lets him know you recognize and honor his feelings. With a gentle yet concerned tone, say, "Alec, you seem upset. I may or may not be picking up your feelings accurately, but I'm wondering if you'd like to talk about it."

Giving a boy who is experiencing strong emotion an opportunity to share his feelings serves as a relief valve to release pressure before it explodes. Don't allow strong emotion to boil over. Avoid an explosion by saying, "Carson, I'm picking up some angry vibes from you. Help me understand what you're feeling."

Anger Management

Anger is a natural human emotion. It's one of the four basic emotions: fear, anger, pain, and pleasure. Perhaps you've heard them expressed as sad, mad, glad, and scared. There is nothing wrong with feeling angry. The problem is not inherent in feeling angry. It manifests by managing angry feelings in inappropriate and ineffective ways.

The goal in teaching boys how to manage their anger is to reduce extreme and often harmful reactions when anger arises. It's okay to be angry, *and* it is not okay to hurt others (either physically or verbally), to hurt yourself, or to destroy property when angry.

Managing anger is an acquired skill. Boys don't learn how to manage anger without specific guidance and instruction. Saying, "You know better than that," may be true, but does your son have the skill to act appropriately in response to what he knows? Applying a consequence such as sitting in a time-out chair, being sent to detention center, or being expelled from school does not teach him how to manage anger nor the skill needed to do something different next time.

Steps in Teaching Anger Management

Step 1: Model the message.

How do you respond when you're angry? Do you scream and yell? Do you throw things or punch holes in walls? Do you cuss and name-call? Do you give others "the silent treatment"? Do you shame, blame, and ridicule? Do you mock or use sarcasm? Do you hit your children or your partner?

How you handle anger demonstrates how you want your children to handle it as well. Model the behavior, words, and tone you want to see them using. Let them hear you say, "I'm angry. I'm going to take a break right now. I'll return in an hour when I've calmed down to discuss this further." When you return, stay in a solution-seeking mode as you strive to reach a resolution.

Step 2: Use the Angry Delivery Statement when expressing your anger.

The Angry Delivery Statement has three important components. All three include a description of what you intend to communicate.

When faced with a boy's behavior and your rising emotion:
1. Describe the situation.
2. Describe how you are feeling.
3. Describe the desired outcome.

The use of the Angry Delivery Statement sounds like this:

"Jack, your new jacket is on the floor. I'm feeling frustrated. It belongs on a hook in the hall."

"Treyvon, I noticed empty pop cans and candy wrappers in the back seat of the car after you returned last night. I'm annoyed because I don't like to drive a messy car. Pop cans and candy wrappers belong in the trash."

"Tevi, I see dirty dishes on the dinner table. I feel resentful. Dirty dishes belong in the dishwasher after they've been rinsed off."

"Jeremy, I found wet towels and a wet floor in the bathroom. My clean socks got soaked. I'm furious. Wet towels belong on the towel rack, and the floor needs to be dry."

"Ian, I heard put-downs in your conversation with your sister. I'm discouraged and annoyed. Conversation in this family needs to be uplifting and affirming."

Please take note, when you're describing the desired outcome you are NOT telling your son what to do. You are using your words to paint a picture of the end result. The choice to do something about it or not is left up to the child. The goal of the Angry Delivery Statement is for you to be able to communicate your feelings clearly and respectfully, not to give orders. You will have time to address his choices when one or both of you are in a calm state of mind.

Step 3: Assess the situation.

When boys are in angry mode, they're not always ready to receive information on how to express their anger effectively. When your son is crying because juice was spilled on the picture he drew and left on the table, he's not emotionally ready to engage in a discussion about feelings. When your teen is distraught because he needs the computer to finish his homework and his brother is using it to play games, it's premature and counterproductive to begin immediately teaching him about expressing his anger with an Angry Delivery Statement. An important role of parents is to help their boys get into a frame of mind that fosters appropriate expression and solution seeking before they begin teaching how to handle anger.

Behavior management, solution seeking, and problem solving take place in an area of the brain called the frontal lobe. This area is the output and control center for behavior. The frontal lobe helps one listen, create choices, choose among options, compare possible outcomes, and manage behavior. When a boy is caught up in strong emotion, it's not the time to give advice, soothe feelings, give constructive feedback, console, or engage in solution seeking. HE CANNOT HEAR YOU!

When your child demonstrates physical behavior such as hitting, kicking, biting, throwing objects, stomping feet, swinging arms, and yelling, "I hate you," he is in tantrum mode. Such behavior is generated in the midbrain, not in the cortex, where the frontal lobe is located. Yelling, screaming, crying, and other emotional behaviors are generated in the limbic brain, which assists in managing emotional content and is not typically a problem-solving area.

As a parent, it's important that you recognize these behaviors and understand that your son is not in an appropriate space to learn anger management skills or listen to problem-solving strategies. Teaching, preaching, reassuring, and problem solving will not work when a boy is drowning in his emotions. The timing is off. When a person in water is going under and flailing around helplessly, it's not the appropriate time to give them swimming lessons. Attempting to instruct or problem solve in the middle of a tantrum or during an emotional outburst will serve no useful purpose. Your role at this time is to help your son pass through the tantrum phase and move into a mode where behavior can be managed and instructions received.

To move a child into his frontal lobe, where he's open to hearing the message you want to deliver, calmly use words to paint a picture of the behaviors or emotions you observe. If your five-year-old is having a tantrum, say what you see or hear. For instance, "Your legs are kicking. Your arms are swinging around. Your teeth are clenched and your body is moving all over the place." If your adolescent son storms out of the computer room slamming the door and announcing how unfair the world is, tell him, "I hear anger in your voice. You seem frustrated. The sound of the door slamming shook the whole house." With a teenager it might sound like this: "You're so upset you can't stop yelling. You look like you want to hit someone. There is fire in your eyes and your jaw is tight. Your voice is getting louder and louder."

Continue to use words that paint a picture of your son's behavior. Be descriptive. Adding judgments and inferences such as "You're being rude" or telling him he's disrespectful will only intensify the tantrum. Somewhere in the process of your describing his behavior, he will give you eye contact. This is a signal that he's beginning to access his frontal lobe. Use this opportunity to suggest a feeling. "You seem really sad." If he retreats into tantrum mode, return to describing what you see and hear. Wait for eye contact and repeat the process as often as necessary until you've engaged a conversation. This parental response helps boys to identify and recognize their own behavior and emotion. As they become aware of their physical movements and feelings, the frontal lobe becomes activated. Then you can move to teaching, debriefing, or accountability.

Some boys move into the mode where behavior management can take place faster than others. For some it could require only seconds, while for others it may take up to thirty minutes. If you give your son whatever time he needs to collect himself, the process of teaching anger management will be more productive and rewarding for both of you.

You are now ready to move to step four.

Step 4: Encourage your son to use Angry Delivery Statements.

When you talk with him about his anger, ask him to describe what he is angry about. Help him use words that describe the situation in as much detail as possible. Descriptions are statements of fact and are void of assumptions or accusations.

"I didn't get a turn on the swing at recess."

"I want to play on the iPad and Jamal won't let me."

"It took me a long time to build my Lego castle and Jeremy knocked it over."

"Rachel keeps coming in my room and won't leave me alone."

Once he has described the situation from his point of view, invite him to express how he's feeling. When needed, help him communicate frustration, irritation, annoyance, and any other forms of anger without judgments or attacking personality or character. Give him some more precise feeling words to use beyond those of mad, pissed, or angry: irritated, disgusted, exasperated, resentful, annoyed, frustrated, discouraged, depressed, impatient, flabbergasted.

Then ask him to describe what he would like to have happen next time: his desired outcome. Remember, he is expressing *his* anger. This is *his* Angry Delivery Statement, not yours. It's important that you let him state what he wants, even if it's not possible for him to have or do that right now. Honor his expression of anger first. There will be time to seek a solution to the problem later. First, focus on teaching him how to express anger effectively.

Step 5: Engage in a solution-seeking process.

The solution-seeking process can be summarized as follows:

1. See the problem as an opportunity to learn and grow.

2. Describe the problem from different points of view.

3. Brainstorm possible solutions.

4. Reach consensus on which solution to use next time.

5. Commit to taking action to bring about the chosen solution.

6. Set a date to evaluate how things are going.

7. Evaluate the effectiveness of the action taken.

When moving through the solution-seeking process with your son, remember that the process is as important as the product. It matters that the specific solution proposed demonstrates empathy and compassion. It also matters that your son learns and becomes comfortable with the process of finding solutions so he can apply the process to future problems he may encounter.

Solution seeking takes time. Yes, it is quicker simply to tell your son what to do. Yes, it is easier to come up with a solution yourself and require that it be implemented. Clearly, it is more efficient to simply tell your son how to behave and expect him to do it. But *efficient* doesn't always equate with *effective*. It is more effective in the long run to involve your son in the search for ways to manage his anger. It is more effective to have boys experience the solution-seeking process than to merely tell them how to solve their problems. If raising caring, empathetic, compassionate boys is your goal, think in terms of being effective, not of being efficient.

Support Assertiveness, Not Aggression

A major difference exists between being assertive and being aggressive. One who is assertive has the qualities of self-confidence, self-assurance, having strong opinions, and stating requests clearly while respecting the feelings, opinions, and rights of others. One who is aggressive also possesses qualities of self-confidence, self-assurance, and having strong opinions. The major difference between being assertive and being aggressive is that aggression has the intent of inflicting damage or hurting another person in order to influence others and have one's needs met. An aggressive person uses hostility, destruction, intimidation, and violence to this end. There is little or no respect for the feelings, opinions, or rights of others. The end result justifies the means, regardless of the cost to others.

Sadly, most boys are being raised to be aggressive, not assertive. They are being taught in a variety of ways to use aggression to create change. When boys are allowed to be pushy or demanding to get their way, they are learning to use aggression to dominate another person. When they're allowed to play violent video games at an early age, they learn that violence is a way to resolve conflict. When parents try to stop their son from being aggressive by overpowering him and taking a position of authority, or by intimidation, they are using a form of aggression as a way to stop aggression. They are teaching their son the very behavior they are trying to eliminate.

Support assertive behavior by:

1. Having regular family meetings where the opinions of all the members are heard and embraced.

2. Asking your son his thoughts and ideas on a home improvement project.

3. Helping your son use a language of boundaries. Teach him to say, "I don't like it when you say those things to me," "I

won't play with you when you treat me that way," "I won't let you do that to me anymore."

4. Encouraging your son to seek the advice of a younger sibling.

5. Letting each child in your family pick one activity that all members will participate in during summer break.

6. Teaching your boys to notice kindness and use their words in appreciation of it.

7. Considering the feelings of others by asking, "What effect do you think that decision will have on your sister or brother?"

8. Letting go of the "Do as I say" attitude.

9. Going to the victim first when aggression happens. Taking care of the victim's hurt or sadness demonstrates that a person's feelings are a priority in your home.

10. Letting your teen offer his opinion on a curfew change when significant social events occur.

11. Teaching your son to say, "I don't understand this," "Can you help me figure this out?" and "Will you explain this to me?"

12. Encouraging your son to speak up and offer possible solutions when problems arise.

13. Frequently asking, "What do you think about that?" "Do you have a different thought about that?" or "What's your opinion?"

14. Teaching your son the difference between getting someone IN trouble and getting them OUT of trouble.

15. Developing a broad-based feeling vocabulary. Teach your son to say, "I'm feeling really frustrated right now," "I get scared when I climb on the roof," or "I'm disappointed that the rain washed out my softball game."

16. Helping your boys learn to describe the behavior they appreciated or tell the effect it had on their lives. "I appreciated it when you helped me clean my room" and "Thank you for buying me the new coat" are examples of describing the behavior.

17. Encouraging your son to tell another person the effect they had on his life and express appreciation. "You saved me an hour in my day. I appreciate that." "Because you helped me, I was able to get all my homework done. Thanks."

18. Giving boys permission to have feelings and teaching them the names for those feelings so they are more likely to articulate them in the future.

19. Using alternatives to yelling, taking an aggressive stance, and spanking.

20. Exploring with your son alternative ways for him to get what he wants.

Life Examples

Fernando Uribe found an empty juice box stuck between the cushions of his brand-new couch. His six-year-old son Martin, who had been snacking on the couch earlier, was now upstairs in his room quietly reading.

As he made his way up the stairs to confront his son, Fernando could feel his irritation rising. When he got close to the door, he remembered the Angry Delivery Statement and its use for communicating strong emotion effectively. He paused for a moment outside his son's door, took a few deep breaths, constructed the three-part message in his head, then knocked on the door.

After being invited in, Fernando told his son directly and firmly, "Martin, I found an empty juice box in the couch. It's still there. I feel mad. Trash belongs in the garbage can under the sink."

With that, he turned and walked away. Shortly, Martin made his way downstairs and took care of the juice box in an appropriate manner.

*****

Jimmy Nelson had saved his lawn-mowing money for several months to purchase a dirt bike he saw advertised in the newspaper. He talked it over with his parents, and they agreed that he could buy the motorcycle and that he would be solely responsible for its upkeep, gas, accessories, and anything else that owning it involved.

After two weeks of riding around the family farm with his friends, Jimmy found himself spending more time trying to keep the dirt bike running than he did riding it. He spent hour after hour almost every day repairing some malfunction. On occasion, days went by without his being able to ride it at all.

With each passing day, Jimmy's frustration and anger grew. His anger would often escalate into screaming, slamming doors, and throwing tools. Every day Mrs. Nelson listened to her son rant, rave, and throw tantrums without saying a word. Finally, feeling something needed to be done, she told her husband the motorcycle had to go.

Mr. Nelson agreed that something needed to be done, but he didn't feel that getting rid of the motorcycle was the best remedy. Instead, he created a space in the barn just for Jimmy's tools and the bike. His parents informed him that any and all things related to fixing it needed to remain in the barn. That included tantrums as well as tools.

It was difficult at times for Jimmy's mother to not step in and take over. She desperately wanted to help her son with his anger. Yet, she was able to confine her interventions and redirection to only those times when his anger spilled outside the barn. She reminded herself frequently that it was not her job to teach this lesson in anger management.

In time, Jimmy's anger diminished. He spent less time in the barn and found other interests with his friends. At the end of the summer, Jimmy asked his dad for help in getting the motorcycle running so he could sell it. For several nights they worked together to get it back in working condition. Jimmy took one last spin around the farm and set the bike out front with a "For Sale" sign on it. On the way back to the house, he said, "Dad, thanks for letting me figure this one out on my own."

Putting his arm around his son, Mr. Nelson replied, "Your mom might appreciate hearing those words too, son."

*****

Tonya and Ray regularly walked their three-year-old son Michael down the driveway to get the mail. Their home was located on a narrow, busy country road where cars reached speeds of fifty to fifty-five miles per hour or more. The mailbox was positioned on the other side of this potentially dangerous road.

The regular mail-collecting ritual was simple and safe. As the family reached the road, one parent would stay behind and hold Michael's hand. The other parent modeled crossing the street safely by looking both ways several times, waiting patiently for all the cars to pass, and staying focused on the task.

One day, as Tonya started across the street, Michael began to scream, "I want to get the mail! I want to get the mail!" and tried to pull away from his father. Ray held firmly to his son's hand and said, "No. It's not safe. Mom will get it and bring it back to us."

Michael threw his body to the ground kicking and screaming. Ray bent down next to his son and said, "You look frustrated. You want to cross the street and get the mail, and I won't let you. Your whole body is showing your anger, and your voice is loud. You're angry." Michael kept on kicking and screaming. Quietly, Ray continued to describe the situation. "I wonder if the people in the cars can hear you as they zoom past. Look, there goes one now. Wow! That was fast." Michael looked up.

Looking up was the signal Ray was watching for. When he observed the slight change in his son's behavior, he quickly picked him up and said, "Michael, I want to keep you safe, and you want to get the mail. Let's go back to the house with Mom, and the three of us will talk about all the ways you can get the mail safely."

Once back at the house, Tonya and Ray talked about the cars on the road and how fast they go. They talked about how difficult it is to see people on the road as they zoom past. They agreed with Michael that he should be able to have a turn to get the mail, and together they brainstormed ideas of how to do that safely.

Michael suggested moving the mailbox. Dad suggested driving up to the mailbox in the car. Mom suggested carrying Michael in her arms as Dad watched closely for cars. With a little guidance and a lot of concern for each other's opinions, Michael chose Mom's idea. With a clear plan articulated and a promise that it would be implemented the next day, Michael smiled and happily ran into the other room to play.

As Michael grew in size and experience, the family revisited the mailbox issue occasionally to explore other safe ways to get the mail. Each time, Michael was an integral part of the decision-making process, and each time he left the discussion with a smile on his face. He felt included, important, and empowered. And he was learning the important life skill of solution seeking.

*****

As Jim walked into the school office, he could hear his son screaming in the adjoining room, "No, I won't go! I won't let go of the desk! Leave me alone!"

The school secretary pointed to the door and mouthed the words, "Go in." Jim opened the door to find his ten-year-old son Tony sitting on the floor holding tightly to the corner of the principal's desk. The exasperated principal stated firmly, "He's suspended. Get him out of here, and don't bring him back for two days!"

The principal handed Jim a suspension slip with a note from Mr. Howard, Tony's teacher, describing what Tony had done. According to the note, Mr. Howard had been called from the room, and when he returned he found Tony standing on a chair "clowning around." The note said that Tony refused to leave the room when he was ordered to go and argued that he was not clowning around. The report went on to say that Tony became disrespectful to the teacher and that was why he was being sent to the office.

The suspension slip also included notes from the principal. He cited Tony's disrespectful behavior in the office, including his loud, argumentative, and angry tone. The principal wrote that Tony refused to sit in the chair as told and that he kept yelling, "I didn't do anything wrong."

After reading the notes on the suspension slip, Jim calmly sat down on the floor next to his son and said, "Tony, tell me what happened from your point of view. How did all this get started for you?"

With tears in his eyes and a cracking voice, Tony explained. "The girl I was sitting next to was having trouble seeing her paper because the sun was shining in her eyes. She tried to close the shade a little, but it got stuck. I stepped up on the chair to fix the shade just as Mr. Howard walked in. He yelled at me right away, saying I knew better than that, and he told me to go out in the hall. He never gave me a chance to explain that I was trying to help. Nobody did." Tony lowered his head and said, "Then I just got mad."

Jim helped his son to his feet and escorted him out the door. As he did, he looked at the principal and said, "I'll be back tomorrow to talk with you further about this incident."

If Mr. Howard had suspended judgment for a brief moment, he could have learned about Tony's intentions. He could even have assisted Tony by holding the chair as Tony released the shade. He could have seized the moment and involved the entire class in brainstorming other ways to solve the problem in a safe and helpful manner.

By suspending judgment, Mr. Howard could have created a different scenario and outcome. Instead, he gave Tony an opportunity to learn how to manage his anger and how to present his opinion effectively to those who are quick to pass judgment.

*****

Two kindergarten students came bursting out of the school bus pushing, shoving, and loudly proclaiming their existence. As they entered the schoolroom door, they continued their struggle. In an instant they were sprawled on the floor kicking, slugging, grabbing, and hollering.

The teacher went immediately to the two boys and separated them with gentle firmness. "I can see you boys are angry," she stated. "It's okay to be angry here." The boys looked at her and nodded. She continued, "Let me show you what you can do with your anger." The teacher then took both boys by the hand and led them to the woodworking center, where she pulled out a box of scrap lumber, some nails, and two hammers. "Now show me just how angry you are by hammering nails into these boards," she challenged.

The boys responded. Angry noise filled the room as hammers alternately hit and missed nails. Several minutes later the nail hammering ended. The boys tired of the task and found other activities to experience.

Later that day, during quiet time, the teacher talked with each boy privately about what happened on the school bus, how he was feeling at the time, and what he could do differently next time when those feelings occur.

Conclusion

We don't have to function with malicious intent to do harm to the development of our boys. The absence of empathy and understanding is enough. It is up to each one of us to create emotional health in our homes. Yes, eliminating empathy deficit in your home might seem overwhelming to you right now, especially if several children are afflicted. Take your time. Move slowly and steadily toward the goal, one feeling word at a time.

Lesson 6: Teaching Cooperation, Not Competition

Our society has become obsessed with the need to be number one. We create ranking systems for everything from reading books in school to science Olympiads to sporting events to movies and music. Being first is the coveted position: first chair in band, first in your class, first in regionals, first in state, first across the finish line, first in the college rankings, first in your age group, first born. First, first, first.

"What's wrong with striving to be first?" you may be asking. "A little healthy competition builds character. Not everyone can be first. We have to prepare our children for the harsh reality that the world is full of losing moments. Competition is the best way to get kids ready for the real world."

What if that is simply not true? What if competition is actually the *worst* way to prepare our kids for a successful life? What if the reason so many people believe that competition is healthy is because they have been heavily influenced by a toxicity that has turned our society into "me first" junkies.

Healthy Competition Is a Contradiction

As a certified sports counselor who has worked with college and professional athletes, I have seen firsthand the destructive nature of competition. The attitude required to be a competitor alienates us from others. When we enter into a competition, we strive to make ourselves right and others wrong. Being right promotes a "me vs. them" attitude. It creates a mental separation which puts distance between us and other people. We constantly judge and compare, resulting in an increased focus on differences, not commonalities. We concentrate on specific incidents that support our judgments and ignore incidents that don't. "Me vs. them" thinking interferes with reaching consensus and destroys feelings of togetherness.

Striving to be "better than" sabotages our ability to see the world from someone else's point of view. Through competition we become less empathetic, less generous, and less able to see from the perspective of others. Our ability to relate to others diminishes significantly, and we adopt separative thinking and antisocial behavior

.

The Poison of Competition

Competition is not the answer; it is part of the problem. Competition is destructive, not healthy. It puts emphasis on power, control, and aggression. It is rooted in making others fail. To be successful, one must triumph over another. To dominate in your field is to be a winner. Being victorious is the apex of success in the mind of the competitor. All at the expense of someone else.

Competition breeds boys who find pleasure in putting others down to build themselves up. A "me vs. you" mentality and social environment is established in which boys learn to beat other children. Through competition, boys discover new ways to take advantage of other children's differences. They become masters at misdirection, intimidation, and coercion. Competition teaches boys to become manipulative, aggressive, dominating men. Manhood is claimed by taking first place over women, children, minorities, or whoever is weaker. That is toxic masculinity.

Striving to be number one becomes the goal. The focus is on the reward, not connection to the people involved or the lessons that can be learned from them. Acquiring the trophy or medal or the top spot on the podium distances the competitor from others and from the resources available in social reciprocity. Through competition, boys are taught that in order to win you must disconnect from others, take advantage of their weakness, cheat whenever possible (a common statement in athletic circles is *If you're not cheating, you're not trying*), and dominate.

Team Competition

What about team competition? Doesn't competing as a team build camaraderie and connection? While it's true that, as a team, players have to learn how to work together, the goal is the same: defeating others. The "we vs. them" mentality is still in play and teaches the same toxic lesson to the individual team members: use power to control, manipulate, and dominate. Even among the members of the team the mentality of "me vs. you" prevails. Teammates battle one another to be a starter, not a bench warmer. Cooperation takes a backseat as individual players skirmish to be in the starting lineup. Boys are still taught that might makes right.

Our boys are growing up in a competitive society. They are being influenced by competition in the classroom, on the playground, in video games, in peer groups, and in the home. It is our responsibility to keep the poison of competition from passing to another generation.

The Antidote

The antidote to the toxicity of competition is cooperation. When we teach boys cooperation they feel a sense of belonging and oneness, they learn to trust others, they demonstrate compassion for the differences of those around them, they communicate openly and honestly, and they value building relationships. As a parent, all that you hope to achieve by putting your boy in competitive situations can be accomplished through teaching cooperation. Where competition puts boys at odds with others, cooperation puts them at one with others.

The key to dissolving competition's contribution to toxic masculinity is developing a sense of oneness. We do this by placing the family first. While independence is important in a boy's development, so too is connectedness and belonging. When boys feel connected to a larger unit (a family), a sense of security is created. They are then safe to explore and challenge themselves independently within the security of the family structure.

Cooperation happens in families when the adults in the family unit work with intentionality to create it. It requires parents who value family unity and place it high on their list of priorities. The family is a place where members experience connectedness, can count on each other, and believe *we're all in this together*.

Consider the following guidelines for helping you teach cooperation and develop a sense of oneness in your family.

<u>Value People over Things</u>

Teach your sons that people are more important than things. As they have the opportunity to feel connected through the support, encouragement, and understanding of others in the family, boys begin to realize that people are valued over objects and rigid rules. Tasks such as making sure the grass is mowed, the house is cleaned, or the garbage is taken out are not as important as playing soccer in the backyard together, listening to your teenage son tell you about his date last night, or rocking your baby to sleep.

When your son hits his younger sister out of frustration and you rush to the aid of your daughter first, you send an important message. When you console her before correcting your son's behavior, you are teaching both of your children that people's feelings have value. You are demonstrating the principle that people are more important than implementing discipline strategies. When you go to your daughter first, your son is not being reinforced for his aggressive behavior but is being shown where value is placed in your family—on the feelings and well-being of individual family members.

A child's motivation to behave does not come from fear of punishment. It comes from being in a relationship. Being connected to a family and feeling that connection in one's heart and soul is what helps a child manage his own behavior. Boys' desire to be a part of the family is strengthened when people are more important than things and the emphasis is on family first.

Connect Emotionally

Feelings are always more important than things. Create an environment where it is safe to be emotional. Encourage the expression of feelings. Allow your feelings to extend to your son as you share traditions, mourn the loss of a loved one, reflect on events from the day's activities, and gather as a family. Demonstrate empathy, compassion, and understanding.

Don't Allow Teasing

Family is a place where teasing about one's hairstyle or recent social blunder is not permitted. Jokes about someone's fears or shortcomings are not tolerated. Members of the family are embraced and celebrated for their differences. Within the security of a loving family, children feel safe to try new things, make mistakes, and discover who they are. You may choose to review "Eliminate Put-downs, Teasing and Name Calling" in Lesson 2.

Define Success

Never link success with winning or losing. Instead, help your son understand what success is and what it is not. Success isn't being victorious over another. It's not about dominance, triumph, or winning. Success has nothing to do with being number one or being better than the other guy.

Success is about discovering your gift and giving it away. You become a successful person when you figure out what you do well and do more of that until that is mostly what you do. The goal is to have a variety of experiences throughout life that help you become aware of who you are as a person and discover what it is that you do well.

You could be involved in a sport, play in the band, join chess club, participate in robotics, be on the student counsel, or perform in the drama club. You can choose to do a myriad of things—not to win at them but to experience them. Through the experience, you gain knowledge and understanding about yourself.

Avoid Comparison

Don't compare your children to one another. Avoid saying things like, "Your brother never acts that way," and "If your sister can do it, why can't you?" When you hold one child up as the model in an attempt to encourage better behavior in a sibling, you're using manipulation to bring about the desired result. You're creating a "better than" scenario. "Better than" thinking builds resentment and divisiveness among your children and sabotages family connectedness.

Don't Run Your House Like a Democracy

In a family, decisions are made with the needs and wants of all in mind. Everyone has input, from the youngest to the oldest, and a decision is reached in the family's best interest. One person doesn't get what they want every time, and the notion that majority rules is not always employed.

Don't run your house like a democracy. Don't put every decision to a vote. If two of the three kids always want to eat out at a pizza place and the third likes Mexican food, the one who likes Mexican food will get out-voted every time. Protect interests of a family voting member who is in the minority by discussing options, considering past choices, and valuing the opinion of each individual.

Use Rituals

An effective way to build feelings of belonging and develop a sense of oneness in your family is through the use of rituals. Rituals embody the myths, history, identity, and purpose of the family. When practiced with frequency and intensity, they create connectedness.

A ritual can be almost any activity the family engages in regularly. It can be big or small. It can be expensive or cost nothing. It can be connected to a holiday or not. What makes an activity a ritual is the repetition and drama that elevates it above ordinary activities. Eating a meal is an everyday activity that can be elevated to ritual status when the family gathers every Sunday morning to eat personalized omelets made to order by Dad. Taking the time to read a book with your child wouldn't be a ritual in and of itself. Reading a chapter in a special book together on Saturday morning becomes a ritual when it occurs regularly over time.

A ritual does not require props, crowds, or special training to perform. Singing a song as you clean up the toys in the playroom could be a ritual. Making popcorn every Friday night as the family sits down to watch a video is a ritual. Saying a special prayer together with your child every night as you tuck him into bed is a ritual. Having a special dinner every time someone has a birthday is a ritual.

Creating a sense of oneness by using rituals involves identifying an activity the family finds enjoyable and repeating it over and over. Search your family life for everyday happenings that are fun, relaxing, creative, exciting, or educational. Can that activity be repeated frequently? If so, it may make a great ritual. Create rituals that are unique to your family. Your children will remember them for the rest of their lives.

Many families have holiday rituals that require extra time and energy that must be shared with everyday tasks and responsibilities. Be present regardless of what you are doing. When they feel pulled in several directions, many parents turn to multitasking. I suggest that you avoid the urge to multitask and instead strive to stay focused on the moment at hand. When you sit with your children, whether it's to play a game or read a book, give them your undivided attention.

Make a "Be" Choice

How you choose to *be* affects whatever you choose to *do*. When you are with your children, choose to be interested in what they're interested in. Choose to be happy that you have the time to focus on their needs and wants. Choose to be excited about the time you have with them. Even when misbehavior occurs, choose to be glad you have the opportunity to help them learn a new behavior or a new way to communicate a desire or express a feeling.

Focus on Listening Rather Than Telling

Children spend a great portion of their day following directions: pick up your clothes, make your bed, sit down, be quiet, go play, chew with your mouth closed, stop picking on your brother, hang up your coat, brush your teeth. The list of commands seems endless. Remember, children have valuable things to say, too. Often parents get so focused on telling that they forget to listen. Value your children's opinion. Allow opportunities to vent. Embrace their point of view. Invite suggestions. Listen to their voice.

Connect Physically

Touch is a powerful way to communicate "I love you." Get close and touch your son's heart with a warm embrace or a gentle squeeze of the shoulder. Snuggle under a blanket and read together. Go for a walk and lock hands. Wrestle on the living room floor. Dispense hugs, smiles, winks, and an occasional high five.

Unplug from the Electronic World

The television set, computer, video games, and tablets have the potential to create a disconnect from personal interaction. Unplug, turn it off, and walk away. While riding in the car, unplug the headphones, turn off the DVD player, and tell your children a story about the day they were born, or share a favorite holiday memory. Shut down the computer, turn off the Xbox, and play a game of chess, checkers, or Catan together. Stand up, walk away from the TV, and go shoot baskets, skip rope, or ride bikes with your son.

Play by the Kids' Rules

Play with your children at their level. Build mud pies, jump in rain puddles, roll down a hill, spray shaving cream on the kitchen table and join in the creation of artistic designs. Cover the driveway in sidewalk chalk. Let your son take the lead and change the rules of a game if he wants. Know that play, no matter how childish or silly it may appear, is an investment in connecting with your children. Play regularly, and remember that the reason for play is to play, not to win.

Preserve Family History

Children require a deep feeling of being connected to their past or heritage in order to sink roots. When these human roots grow deep, they hold the child firm, creating stability.

Begin by keeping a recorded history of your family. Take photos and arrange them chronologically. A shoebox or desk drawer doesn't work. More organization is needed for this purpose. Large photo albums work well. Along with photos of vacation trips, birthdays, athletic events, and other significant occasions, mix in samples of schoolwork, postcards from grandparents, or printed memorabilia from events you've attended together.

When several albums have accumulated, display them in a place of importance in your home. This "nostalgia corner" can be enhanced by adding baby books, memorabilia, and journals. It's also an ideal place to store family folklore, including the myths, folktales, or special stories pertinent to your family. Invite your own parents to record memories from their lives so their stories can be preserved.

Create a file of schoolwork for each child to add to your nostalgia corner. By preserving special papers in a systematic way, children can return to them repeatedly over time to see their growth. When they look at their work on math problems, creative writing, or penmanship on a daily basis, it's difficult for them to notice growth and improvement. Seeing the products of their work over time allows them to observe their progress and accomplishment.

Life Examples

Arthur had an appointment with a local attorney to discuss a legal matter regarding his hunting lodge property. Not totally trusting lawyers, he didn't look forward to their first meeting.

When he entered Mr. Tillman's office, Arthur noted the professional credentials and diplomas on the wall. He was impressed by the massive display of the lawyer's accomplishments and felt intimidated until a mahogany plaque in the middle of all the other neatly framed items caught his eye. It was inscribed with the words: SUCCEED AT HOME FIRST.

Arthur began to relax. He liked the fact that the plaques informing clients of Mr. Tillman's professional accomplishments were placed around the one that told of the importance of his family. Arthur knew then that their professional relationship would be long and mutually satisfactory.

*****

Steven's stepfather, Jerry Dyer, travels frequently as part of his profession. While away, he stays connected to his stepson by using one of his passions, horses.

Whenever he is off on a business trip, Jerry finds a postcard of a horse and mails it to his stepson along with a warm greeting. Sometimes he gets home before the postcard arrives. At other times, the postcard beats him.

Over the past five years, Steven has filled a shoebox with horse postcards. They show pictures of Arabians, Quarter Horses, Appaloosas, and Morgans, as well as other breeds. The cards also include pictures of Native Americans, jockeys, farmers, soldiers, fox hunters, and cowboys. Some horses are full grown. Others are foals. Some are wild. Others are domesticated.

At last count, Steven had accumulated 317 postcards of horses, each with a message from his stepfather. On occasion, Steven and Jerry take the postcards out and organize them on the kitchen table. They make a pile of their top ten favorites and take turns telling why they selected each one. They talk about the funny ones and what it might be like to live in the period of time or part of the country shown on the postcard.

Home or away, the horse postcards help Steven and his stepdad connect.

*****

Some parents see New Year's Eve as an opportunity to get away from the family to celebrate in private or with friends. Going out to dinner, attending parties, and emptying bottles seems to be the order of the night. Another alternative, one that can help your family grow closer, is to spend New Year's Eve together. That's what the Lowrys do. They see New Year's Eve as an ideal time to celebrate connectedness, reflect on the past year, and look ahead to the future.

For the Lowrys, deciding what treats to purchase, shopping together, and decorating as a family occupy much of the day. Dinner and card games fill the early evening. When interest in games dies down, they assemble in the living room, sit in a circle, and begin the most meaningful part of their New Year's Eve together: Topic Talk.

Topics are ideas they dream up to structure the family conversation. One family member suggests a topic like "A new friend I made this year" or "My favorite song this year." The Lowrys then each take a turn responding to the topic for as long as they wish. Listeners do simply that—listen. When each person has had an opportunity to respond to the topic, family members ask questions and elaborate on their remarks. Topics used in the past that have helped the Lowrys get in touch with each other and reflect on the previous year include: "My favorite book this year," "Something I did that I'm proud of," "Something I wish I could do over," "My favorite place I visited this year," "Something I bought for myself," "Something I did for others."

At eleven o'clock, the Lowrys end Topic Talk and get out Our Goals, a list of goals the family shared and recorded a year earlier. Each member takes a turn reading his or her goals from the preceding year and telling whether or not they were accomplished. One New Year's Eve the goals were:

Jerry: Go to horseback riding camp.

Matt: Join the drama club and participate in a play.

Brenda: Get my driver's license.

Mr. Lowry: Run a marathon with dignity.

Mrs. Lowry: Lose thirty pounds.

After sharing how they did on the previous year's goals, the Lowrys create new goals for the coming year. Jerry acts as recorder and takes down each family member's contribution. The goals are then put away until the next New Year's Eve celebration.

As the time nears midnight, the Lowrys turn on the TV and count down the minutes and seconds until the New Year arrives. The traditional hugs, kisses, and noisemaking follow.

*****

When Mr. Ashcroft's two sons were in fifth and sixth grades, both of their teachers commented on the sad state of the boys' penmanship. Being a former teacher himself, Mr. Ashcroft believed that one of the best ways to improve penmanship is to practice, but he didn't want his children to sit and do formal penmanship sessions, forming the same letters over and over. So he offered his sons a deal. He agreed to extend each child's bedtime by a half hour if they would agree to write in a journal for ten minutes of the extended time. They agreed. Spiral notebooks were purchased for the project.

Each night, when the boys finished writing, they would bring their journals to their father before they went to bed. Later that night, he would write a few sentences in response and leave the journals by their bedroom door for them to find in the morning. This journal activity was not used to correct spelling or punctuation, or to comment on penmanship. It was used as a time to build relationships. It was a way to connect.

When penmanship became sloppy, Mr. Ashcroft would write, "I can't make this out. What were you trying to communicate here?" He did not write, "This is sloppy."

Mr. Ashcroft found that his children would often put in writing what they would not say aloud. Responding in journals gave him an opportunity to think through what he wanted to say and to share parts of himself with his children.

Over time, the boys' penmanship improved. So did the relationship between a father and his sons.

*****

Thomas took his two sons to school every morning, and he was not enjoying it. Neither, it seemed, were the boys. The twenty-minute ride would begin with an argument about who would sit where. It continued with further arguments about what song to listen to on the radio or who saw the yellow truck first or what was the best topping on a pizza.

One day, in the midst of his sons' arguing over what type of animal was smaller, a vole or a shrew, Thomas interjected, "I know a story about a vole and a mouse and a big barn cat." The excitement in their father's voice caught the boys' attention.

Thomas began to create a scene off the top of his head, telling the story as he drove. Not knowing their father was making up the story as it unfolded in his mind, the boys grew quiet and listened. Encouraged by their apparent interest, Thomas kept adding to the tale until they reached the school. To inspire further interest, he ended the story in mid-sentence with the mouse trapped in a corner by the barn cat. "I guess we'll have to hear the rest tomorrow," he teased.

To Thomas's surprise, the next morning the boys were sitting quietly in the back seat when he got into the car. He barely made it to the end of the driveway before the older one broke the silence. "Well," he said, "tell us the rest of the story. What happens to the mouse?" Thomas smiled and picked up the story where he had left off the day before.

From that day on, every morning on the way to school, Thomas told another part of the mouse story. The boys became so involved they began offering ideas for new storylines and making suggestions for new characters. By the end of the school year, Thomas and the boys had created over twenty-five new animal characters and many additional adventures of Fred, the mouse.

Thomas and his sons wrote down the stories they created on the way to school and have published a series of chapter books for first- and second-grade readers titled *Fred the Mouse*.

*****

Following the remodeling of their home, Clark and Susan Ricket decided that extra care would be needed to maintain the new wood floor. They called a family meeting to discuss the matter and develop a plan that would be easy for the entire family to implement.

During the meeting, all three children and their parents agreed that the new wood floor was beautiful and that changes would need to be made to preserve its luster. They discussed how frequently it should be swept and washed, as well as the use of toys on the floor. It was agreed upon by all that shoes would no longer be worn in the house, and a spot was created by the back door for everyone's outdoor footwear.

A few days later, four-year-old Hunter, the youngest member of the Ricket family, asked to have another family meeting about the wood floor. That evening all five members gathered to hear Hunter's concerns.

"I keep slipping on this floor," Hunter told them.

"Take your socks off," his older brother, Andrew, suggested.

"But my feet will get cold."

"You could wear your slippers, as long as you didn't wear them outside, too," his mother told him.

"Hey, can we all get nice indoor slippers to wear?" asked Darlene, the middle child.

"I don't see why not," Mr. Ricket responded. "We'll all go slipper shopping this weekend."

The following Saturday afternoon, as planned, the family ventured out together in search of the perfect slippers for each person. After they had all made their selections, everyone went home excited about trying out their footwear purchases on the new floor. The slippers were a huge success. Slipping on the floor was effectively eliminated.

Two weeks passed, and Hunter again asked to hold a family meeting about the wood floor. When they gathered, he expressed his concern about having guests at the house. "When other people come to our house, they won't have slippers to wear. They might slip and fall," he said.

"What can we do about that?" Mrs. Ricket asked.

"We can buy a bunch of slippers and keep them in a box by the door," Darlene suggested.

"That would be a lot of slippers to buy to get a size for everyone," their father noted.

"Maybe we shouldn't enforce the 'no shoes' rule for guests who are concerned about slipping on the wood floor," Andrew offered.

Everyone agreed with Andrew's idea, knowing the family placed great value on both safety and having people feel comfortable while in their home.

Hunter, for the time being, was satisfied with the wood floor situation. Everyone knew that if his satisfaction changed, he would be calling another family meeting in the future.

Conclusion

The hierarchical arrangement of families in our society where the man is considered the head of the household, the woman is in charge of the children, the oldest child has say over the younger siblings, and so on down the line creates a feeling of being ruled over, not included in. Developing a sense of oneness in the family where we all work together to support, uplift, and encourage each person's success establishes an attitude of cooperation. Cooperation neutralizes the harmful effects of competition.

You can strengthen family unity and help your sons develop cooperation as a life skill whether you are a single parent, live with a spouse of fifteen years, or see your children only on weekends. You can neutralize the toxicity of competition by producing a sense of oneness and connectedness in your family.

Lesson 7: Teaching Beyond Tolerance

In 1996, the United Nations General Assembly designated November 16 as the International Day of Tolerance. Every year on the sixteenth of November people from all over the world gather to promote tolerance, respect, appreciation, and cooperation amongst the world's different cultures.

Tolerance refers to the recognition and acceptance of appearance, opinions, beliefs, and practices that differ from our own. It is considered the backbone of human rights and fundamental freedoms because people are naturally different. Bringing awareness to the intolerance people demonstrate toward differing ethnic groups is vital in dissolving toxic masculinity. The focus of our white, male-dominated culture is on rejecting those who are outside the norm. Diversity is seen by many as a weakness and a blemish on our society. Standard behavior is to not accept people for who they are and to treat those with different opinions, skin tone, or language as inferior.

My position is that to change the toxicity of our society we need to start by addressing the toxic manifestation of power, manipulation, and control in our homes. We need to promote tolerance not by recognizing an annual day of tolerance but by living a tolerant life. Let our children see us being tolerant of others, including them. The level of tolerance we manifest sets the standard for them. Your son will adopt the values and attitudes you reveal to him through your behavior. He is watching your every move, hearing your tone, and sensing your body language. Where tolerance is concerned, you are the message.

Teaching Tolerance Is Not Enough

To just tolerate another's looks, opinions, beliefs, and practices that differ from our own falls short of what is needed. The word *tolerance* fails to achieve the depth a boy or man needs to explore within himself about what it means to be tolerant. Toxic masculinity has distorted the nature of tolerance. A man influenced by the dominant attitudes of masculinity can tolerate something by ignoring it. He can tolerate a culture by staying away from it and not exposing himself to what it has to offer. He can tolerate someone's behavior by putting up with it but without addressing what the behavior means to the person exhibiting it and what it brings to society. He hides under this altered sense of tolerance, refusing to interact with those who have a different appearance, cultural background, life experience, or value system.

Teaching tolerance is not enough. It's the place to start, *and* we must move beyond mere tolerance if our goal is to raise boys to become empathetic, compassionate men. It is time to move beyond tolerance—way beyond tolerance—to an active appreciation and celebration of differences.

Tolerance and Beyond

The first step is to move the focus from tolerance to acceptance. From there we are in position to push on to the next level: appreciation. Now we're one step away from the top level: celebration.

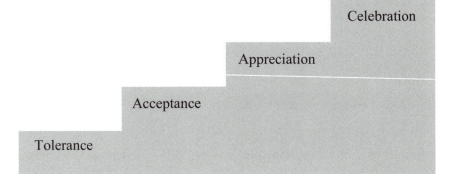

What if we taught our boys how to move up this staircase in our own homes? Yes, our society needs to move beyond mere tolerance. So do other countries and cultures, as do different races and religions. Bosses and employees, the rich and the poor, male and female, and political parties would benefit from a heartfelt dose of expanded tolerance. Still, what if we began in our own homes, with our own children? What would that look like? Where might we begin?

Expanding Tolerance

Step 1: We begin by modeling basic tolerance. As parents, professional educators, coaches, and other adults who work with boys, it's imperative that we go beyond just tolerating a person's unique beliefs or opinions. Start with kindness and politeness even if your internal reaction is fear or disdain when you encounter someone who appears different. Demonstrate respect for their differences.

Words that demonstrate tolerance:

- "That's one way of looking at it."
- "You have an opinion I hadn't thought of."
- "You bring a different perspective to the group."
- "Thank you for joining us today."
- "I'm interested in your point of view."
- "What are some of your family traditions?"

Step 2: In this step we exhibit a level of acceptance by not judging as good or bad a cultural norm that is different from our own. When we encounter a culture or principle that we don't understand, we learn more about it before we establish an uninformed opinion. We share what we learn with our children and teach them how to explore cultural differences and why that exploration and the resulting discoveries are important to our family.

We generally don't have enough information to make accurate judgments about cultural differences. Teach your son that when he judges another person, he judges them on the basis of insufficient evidence. Help him appreciate that he doesn't fully know what it's like to be in the other person's skin. He can't see life through their eyes because he hasn't lived their experiences.

- Talk about stereotypes in the media that inaccurately portray and judge minorities.
- Point out the inappropriate use of stereotypes whenever you hear or see them being used.
- Share what you know about a culture or ethnic tradition as accurately as possible.

- Answer your son's questions about a culture with factual information. If you don't know the answer, research it together.
- Learn together about holiday and religious celebrations that are not part of your own tradition.
- Give your son opportunities to play with others who are different from him.
- Choose a school, day camp, or child-care facility for your son that has a diverse population.
- Select books, toys, music, art, and videos that come from cultures different from those of your family.

Step 3: Step 3 is demonstrating that we understand and appreciate cultural and ethnic differences. In our families we can show appreciation for a different culture or belief by talking about how a diverse population with different cultures enriches our community with new experiences and new ideas. One example would be the wide variety of restaurants we have in our home area. Point out how these restaurants give us new culinary experiences when we frequent them. Without that type of adventure we would have no new data to help us understand and appreciate differences.

- Focus on learning together about other cultures and traditions. Involve your family in situations where diversity is demonstrated, such as religious ceremonies, parades, sporting events, birthday celebrations, or holidays.
- Create an atmosphere of intrigue as you explore how different cultures handle life's occasions in their own special way.

- Debrief your experiences by talking about what each person in your family enjoyed and appreciated about the activity.

- Compare and contrast your own family traditions with the family traditions of various cultures, discussing the similarities and the differences noted.

- Stress the value that diversity brings to your community and home through the experiences you've encountered.

Step 4: In this step we celebrate cultural differences by embracing, uplifting, and sharing aspects of a different culture with our family, perhaps by pointing out all the different cultures that exist in our area. That might include a German, a Polish, a Jewish, a Hispanic, a Muslim, an African-American, and an Asian community. Talking about each culture and acknowledging and honoring what it brings to our community moves us well beyond tolerance on the acceptance staircase. As their understanding and appreciation of other cultures grows, boys will move beyond basic tolerance into the higher levels of appreciation and celebration.

- Invite families from other cultures into your home and share your family traditions with them.

- Honor the religious holidays of other cultures by learning about them and perhaps adopting one of their practices.

- Join a holiday celebration of a family from another culture. Spend the day together sharing their holiday experience with your family and learning about the cultural significance of this day for their family.

- Once a month choose a cultural dish from another country. Research, shop and cook that dish together as a family. While enjoying the meal, talk about the history of the country and the people who live there.

- Identify ways in which a diverse culture has touched your family and influenced your way of living.

- Consider the ways in which cultures have combined and blended in your community, creating a new look to both cultures and the neighboring environment.

Diversity in Your Own Family

Be mindful of the diversity that exists within your own family. "We are all the same race, religion, and beliefs in this family," you might argue. Really? What about the child who moves at a slower pace than other family members? What about the one in a sports-oriented family who would rather read books and play the violin? What about the relative who is gay? How are you going to help your family members not only tolerate differences in siblings and relatives but move to acceptance, appreciation, and celebration?

Consider using the examples below to guide you from intolerance through the four levels of tolerance.

Example 1: Consider the child who prefers a slow pace to life.

Intolerance: Sometimes communicated through ridicule and shame for him being soooo sloooow. You tease him and give him a nickname like "slowpoke" or "turtle." You often confront him about being behind everyone else. You create exercises for him to learn how to "pick up the pace."

Tolerance: You recognize that your child is slow. You may find yourself somewhat irritated with him pace but have chosen to let him deal with the consequences of being slow on his own. You tell him that he gets to walk at his own pace but you are not going to wait for him.

Acceptance: You acknowledge your child's pace for what it is. It is neither good nor bad, right nor wrong. It just is. Your desire is to learn more about how his pace serves him and how he feels when he is pressured to go faster. You encourage him to speak up when the pace feels too fast and to make changes in his life to accommodate his pace.

Appreciation: You see value in the pace that is natural for your child. You walk with him at his pace and feel what he feels. You notice how you can take in more details or focus on a fine point when your pace is slower. His unique pace is appreciated for the new experiences it brings and reduced stress it offers.

Celebration: You honor his pace by giving it a special and positive name, such as *Zachary's Pace* or *Logan Time*. Use that name when it would be important for others to consider a similar pace. You schedule specific events with that pace in mind. You plan for family days where that pace is embraced and used to balance fulfilling work, relaxing play, and opportunities for inspiration and renewal.

Example 2: Consider the child who doesn't like sports in an athletic-minded family.

Intolerance: The child is coerced into participating in youth sports against his personal desires. He is repeatedly admonished to "try harder" and "stay focused." He may be given extra batting practice whether he wants it or not. Frustration grows for all parties involved. Book reading or violin practice may be mocked or put down.

Tolerance: You put up with the fact that your child doesn't like sports, but still judge it internally and silently wish he wasn't that way. You don't quite respect his different interests, yet you don't say much about it. You simply ignore it as best you can.

Acceptance: You realize that it is what it is, and it's probably not going to change. You begin to pay closer attention to your child's interests and start learning more about them. As you learn more, you begin to understand and feel a sense of approval of your child's differing abilities, interests, and style.

Appreciation: You begin to value the way your child plays the violin. You recognize and appreciate what this difference means to you and what it brings to your family. Through the uniqueness of this valued member of your family you encounter new experiences and new ideas that enrich your life and the lives of other family members.

Celebration: In this stage the family goes out to dinner after the violin concert to celebrate the child's musical accomplishments. He becomes the center of attention for the night. You video his concert the same way you did his siblings' soccer games. You play the recording in his presence, describing what you enjoyed about it. You brag about how many books he has read to your friends and other relatives. You let him overhear you telling his grandfather what a voracious reader he is.

Example 3: Consider the child who is gay or lesbian.

Intolerance: You refuse to recognize your child's same-sex orientation and you strongly disapprove. You attempt to convince them they are wrong, sinful, or confused. You want to "fix" them and may even kick them out of your home and not speak to them until they change. Sometimes you feel guilty and think you are somehow responsible. You pray to God to be spared this terrible situation.

Tolerance: Being tolerant of your child's sexual orientation means that you recognize their same-sex orientation, and you may or may not approve. You are no longer in denial. There may be a hint of judgment or misunderstanding, and you do your best to not say much about it. You attempt to not speak negatively about it and might not address it at all.

Acceptance: Being accepting of your child's sexual orientation means accepting that what is, is. You want to learn more about their feelings and experiences. You encourage them to talk with you, and you approach them with an open, loving heart void of judgment.

Appreciation: You value this child's presence in your life and enjoy their perspective and outlook on life. Being appreciative of your child's sexual orientation means recognizing how their involvement in your life enriches your family and your community. You feel connected to them and want them to participate in family functions as much as possible. You simply enjoy who they are and appreciate who they are.

Celebration: Celebrating your child's sexual orientation means you honor their presence in the family. You invite their chosen partner to join your family for Thanksgiving dinner. You encourage the two of them to sit with you at church. Their partner's family history is recorded alongside yours. Your heart is filled with joy when you see them together. You hug them both regularly and tell them, "I love you."

You may be familiar with the notion "Think globally. Act locally." That philosophy fits nicely with tolerance. Think multiculturally as you plan family functions. Think of the big picture in your family snapshot. Level up! Move beyond tolerance. Appreciate and celebrate differences in their many forms. Indeed, the entire world needs it. Why not begin with your family? Today.

Life Examples

Brandon Haslette was given three tickets to a Michigan State football game. Since his wife had no interest in football, he invited his thirteen-year-old son Matt to accompany him and asked Matt to invite one of his friends. Matt had three close friends, all responsible youngsters whom Brandon would be happy to include in their Saturday football adventure.

Three days later, Matt approached his dad and announced, "I have a problem. I don't know who to invite to the football game. I have three good friends, and I can't make up my mind."

Brandon had an adult solution to the problem. He wanted to suggest that Brandon ask Steve. Steve had invited Matt to two Detroit Red Wing games previously, and Brandon wanted Matt to learn a lesson about returning favors, giving back, and remembering those who have helped you in the past. But he didn't suggest Steve. Instead, Brandon bit his tongue and said, "Why don't you check it out inside?"

Matt knew what "check it out inside" meant. His parents had used that phrase with him many times before. It meant go to your room, turn off anything that makes noise, sit quietly, and see if you can get in touch with an inside feeling. It was his job to check in and listen for his own right answer.

While Matt checked it out inside, Brandon reminded himself that his son didn't need to learn the lesson of payback in this moment. He knew that parenting provides many opportunities for parents to teach lessons and that he would get many more opportunities to help Matt learn about remembering past kindnesses. "Better," he thought to himself, "that I use this opportunity to give Matt an experience with trusting his own judgment."

Fifteen minutes later Matt appeared and announced, "It's all set. I invited Charlie, and he accepted." Matt hadn't picked Steve. As they talked about Matt's selection, Brandon found out that Charlie rarely got to do anything special, and Matt's other two friends had parents who arranged frequent interesting adventures for their children. Matt felt it was time for Charlie to have a turn at doing something exciting.

"How did you realize that Charlie needed to do something exciting?" Brandon asked his son. "It just came to me as I sat there in my room," Matt said. "It was a feeling I got, and you always tell me I can trust that. So I did."

Brandon smiled and remembered how he had almost suggested Steve an hour earlier. He gave Matt a pat on the back as they parted, and then gave another to himself for being alert and wise enough to suggest that Matt check it out inside.

*****

Tim has high-functioning autism. He was diagnosed with Asperger's syndrome while he was in second grade.

Two things concerned his teachers as Tim moved through the grades: one, his antisocial behavior, and two, his fascination with birds. The teachers, staff, and administration found it difficult to work with Tim because all he talked about was birds. If a math problem didn't include birds, Tim paid little attention to it. If a story was read that didn't include birds, Tim appeared disinterested.

If you wanted to know anything about birds, Tim was the person to talk to. Even at the age of eight he had a vast knowledge about birds. He could tell you the eating habits, mating rituals, and migratory patterns for birds anywhere in the world.

The other students teased Tim and called him "The Birdman," which didn't bother him because he loved birds so much and took it as a compliment.

A local farmer who had a son in Tim's class heard about his struggles in school and his interest in birds. He stopped by Tim's house one Sunday afternoon to talk with Tim and his mother. He had a few chickens roaming around the farm that provided his family with fresh eggs. He offered to give Tim a couple of baby chicks to raise on his own. Tim was thrilled with the offer and immediately started designing and building a coop. The following week the farmer and his son returned with three baby chicks. The farmer was impressed with Tim's chicken coop design and was pleased to see his enthusiasm. Tim became even more focused on birds and glowed whenever he talked about his chickens.

A problem developed when the teachers thought it would be best for Tim to learn about other aspects of the world in addition to birds. He was forced to put his bird books away. He was disciplined when he refused to participate in classroom activities. He was recommended for special education classes because he wouldn't write his spelling words or complete his math assignments.

Completely frustrated with the approach the school system was taking with her son, Tim's mother decided to begin a homeschooling program. This was a difficult decision for her because she was a single parent who worked fifty hours a week to support her family. Yet, this parent felt something else needed to be done. What the school was doing was clearly not working.

With the encouragement of family and friends, Tim's mother finally removed him from school in the fifth grade. Armed with current research on Asperger's syndrome, she decided to allow Tim's passion for birds to direct his learning. She would let him give his full attention to his chickens.

Five years later, Tim is still "The Birdman." And quite a birdman he is! With the help of the farmer and his son, Tim started his own business supplying local meat markets with organically raised chickens and fresh brown eggs. Because of Tim's successful business, his mom has been able to retire from her day job. She now works for Tim, delivering chickens and eggs to his customers. Not bad for a fifteen-year-old who likes birds.

*****

"I hate Juan," seven-year-old Pablo announced at the dinner table. "He's so stubborn."

"I thought he was your best friend," Pablo's mother said.

"Not anymore. I've never seen anyone so thickheaded."

"I wonder if there isn't another way to see that," his mother suggested.

"What do you mean?"

"I mean, what if you saw 'stubborn' through a different set of glasses?"

"Huh?"

"Like when you put on sunglasses or 3-D glasses everything looks different. Sometimes when you see things through different lenses they don't look the same."

"Mom, you're not making sense. Give me an example."

"What if you were wearing your 'friend' glasses or your 'he's on my side' glasses?" Pablo's mother offered. "What if Juan stubbornly stood up for you in an argument? What if he was using that same stubborn attitude in that situation? How would 'stubborn' look then?"

"Then it wouldn't be so bad, I guess."

"What if he wanted to finish something and stubbornly worked on it until he completed it? Maybe 'stubborn' could be seen as 'determined' in that situation."

"I guess. Have we got extra pie tonight?"

"Why?"

"I thought I'd call Juan and see if he wants to come over."

"Yes, we have plenty, unless he stubbornly eats the whole thing!"

"Oh, Mom!" Pablo said with a grin.

*****

Sam was a seven-year-old bug fanatic. He loved to hunt for bugs in the dirt, discover spiders in their webs, and watch ants as they dragged a leaf across the sidewalk.

One evening while playing with his older brother, Sam spotted a huge spider in the middle of a new web on the bottom of the swing set. "Avery, come look at this spider," he called. A bug lover himself, Avery came running over.

"Let's feed it and watch what happens," his brother suggested, and raced off to find spider food. He found an ant on the sidewalk nearby. Seconds later he returned and tossed a black ant into the web.

Within seconds the spider zipped across the web, grabbed the ant, and began wrapping it tightly in its web. The ant suddenly became motionless as the spider stood over its prey. The entire ordeal took less than ten seconds.

As the two children stood quietly staring at the web, their father looked up from weeding the rock garden. Sensing emotion in their silence, he quickly moved across the yard to them. "What's happening?" he asked.

"We fed the spider," Sam told him. "But I didn't like it."

"You look sad and surprised. Did something happen that you didn't expect?"

"Yeah, I thought it would be a good idea to feed the spider, but as soon as the ant stopped moving I thought that it wasn't a good idea for the ant."

"Yes, Sam," his father acknowledged. "At that moment you felt sad for the ant. Then the sadness surprised you because you didn't expect to feel that way. You felt sadness and surprise together. It's okay to feel sad, and it's important to talk about your feelings so you can understand them better." He paused for a moment, looking at the sadness on both of his children's faces, then added, "Let's go sit on the porch swing for a few minutes and just let our feelings be what they are as we sit together."

*****

As an adjunct professor at the local university, Angelique Howard was involved in the professor exchange program. Each new school year brought a different professor from countries worldwide to teach classes in their respective expertise for an entire school year. The professors would routinely be accompanied by their spouse and children. Angelique helped the families adjust to the cultural changes and get settled into their new surroundings.

Angelique and her husband Trey used this opportunity to create a unique holiday experience for their two boys. It had begun when their oldest son was only two years old. The Howards invited a Japanese professor and her family to join them for a traditional Christmas celebration at their home. A typical meal was prepared, the history of their Christmas tradition was explained, music was played, and gifts were exchanged. That first year left such an impression on both families that Angelique and Trey continued year after year sharing their Christmas with visiting professors and their families. The tradition grew from sharing Christmas to learning about and celebrating the holiday traditions of the other families as well.

Year after year the Howard family celebrated the holiday traditions of families from around the world. Their typical Christmas turned into sharing religious traditions and holiday celebrations with families from Egypt, Saudi Arabia, Bahrain, Sudan, England, Mexico, Germany, France, Japan, and New Zealand. After the Howards heard the history of the tradition of the visiting professor's country, they and the guest family together prepared the customary meal of their guests' country and celebrated as one big family, connecting the two families and their religious differences.

The Howard boys are now young adults living on opposite sides of the United States, and the Howard family still gets together over the holidays. Each year they pick a different country or state in which to meet and create a new holiday experience, local traditions and all. So far they've met in Hawaii, Puerto Rico, Paris, and Spain, and celebrated on a sailboat in the Gulf of Mexico.

At the end of the last trip they began planning how to continue their holiday tradition as their family begins to expand. Trey and Angelique's oldest son has met a partner who is from the Philippines.

Conclusion

First and foremost, model tolerance, which is more than just putting up with someone's differences. As adults, we must demonstrate to boys through our actions that we accept those differences. If we don't understand something about a culture or belief, we seek to learn more about it before we establish an opinion. We share what we are learning with our sons and teach them how to explore cultural differences. We show appreciation for a different culture or belief by pointing out how that culture enriches our community with new experiences and new ideas. We celebrate what each culture brings to our community. The more we engage our family in this practice, the more our boys grow beyond just tolerance and into appreciation and celebration.

Lesson 8: Teaching Sex and Sexuality

Being taught about both sex and sexuality is a crucial part of a boy's development. It's a lesson you need to teach whether you want to or not. It is simply not enough to talk about different body parts when boys are young, how babies are made when they are adolescents, and how to protect themselves from sexually transmitted infections when they are teens. Yes, boys need to be taught body differences, what "having sex" really means, and how to protect themselves from infections and unwanted pregnancy. But there is so much more that parents and professional educators need to be teaching boys: differences in sexual expressions and desires; how one sees oneself as a sexual or nonsexual being; how connected one feels to one's gender, and how the binary male/female classification is not accurate for many people.

The bottom line is this: boys will learn about sex and sexuality whether you talk openly about it with them or not. They're going to obtain sexual information somewhere. It's far better that the information comes from you than from television, music, or their peers. Our male-dominated society is so contaminated by the poison of misogyny that boys are being raised to become men who believe that being misogynistic is part of being a real man. Out of this attitude has arisen a toxicity that is called Rape Culture.

What Is Rape Culture?

Rape culture is a term that refers to a sociocultural environment in which rape and sexual violence is normalized and excused in the media and popular culture. It is perpetuated through the use of misogynistic language, the objectification of women's bodies, and the glamorization of sexual violence. Rape Culture is the mark of a society that creates prejudice against and distrust of women and that disregards women's rights and safety. It has permeated our society at both the individual, one-on-one, level and the institutionalized, structured level.

What Rape Culture Looks Like

1. Blaming the victim. ("She asked for it!")
2. Trivializing sexual assault. ("Boys will be boys!")
3. Speaking about grabbing a woman's private parts and later dismissing it as "locker room talk."
4. Telling sexually explicit jokes.
5. Laughing at rape jokes or comedy sketches.
6. Using the word *rape* in other contexts, such as, "The wind raped my hair," or "That spicy sandwich I just ate raped my stomach." Using the word rape in other than a sexual context trivializes the impact it has on rape victim's lives.

7. Engaging in street harassment or catcalling; telling victims they are "overreacting" when they confront it.

8. Tolerating sexual harassment.

9. Assuming that false reporting of sexual assault cases is the norm. False reporting occurs in 5-8 percent of sexual assault cases.

10. Publicly scrutinizing a victim's dress, mental state, motives, and history and claiming it to be part of the problem.

11. Defining "manhood" as dominant and sexually aggressive.

12. Defining "womanhood" as submissive and sexually passive.

13. Pressuring men to "score."

14. Pressuring women to not appear "cold."

15. Assuming that only promiscuous women get raped.

16. Assuming that men don't get raped or that only "weak" men get raped.

17. Refusing to take rape accusations seriously.

18. Focusing sexual assault prevention education programs on teaching women to avoid getting raped instead of on teaching men not to rape.

19. Allowing politicians to make a distinction between criminal rape and "legitimate rape."

20. Supporting athletes who are charged with rape and label their victims "career destroyers."

Society is going to have an influence on the sexual development of your son, and if you leave it up to someone else to teach him about sex and sexuality, you greatly increase the potential for his growing up to be a chauvinistic, misogynistic, bigoted man who believes that he isn't any of those things.

Reclaiming Your Role as Sex Educator

Reducing sexual harassment and misogynistic behavior cannot and must not come from calling upon girls and women to change. Suggesting that women need to change in any way implies that a man's misogynistic behavior is women's fault.

The problem needs to be resolved at the family level. Parents need to reclaim their role as sex educator. But many parents aren't sure what to say, when to say it, or how to say it. Some parents avoid talking with their boys about sexuality as long as possible. Others freeze up when it comes to answering sex-related questions. Parents worry about saying the wrong thing, giving too much information, or creating unhealthy curiosity.

Communication between parent and child is the key component in raising sexually healthy and responsible boys who become healthy masculine men. Reclaiming your role as sex educator requires that you take the lead in opening a discussion about sex with your children. You will need to be alert for teachable moments and be ready to talk and listen.

Removing Obstacles Parents Face

Below are the six most frequent obstacles parents face when talking to their boys about sex and sexuality, along with strategies to overcome them. Use these suggestions to help you ease any fear you might be feeling and to help you find the words to talk to your son about sexuality, the poison of misogyny, and the devastating effects of rape culture.

Obstacle 1: Fear of harming your son

No one worries that the information children get in driver education classes will lead to more accidents. No one is concerned that if children are taught about nutrition they will ruin their health by eating too much of the wrong foods. Yet, many parents fear that talking about sex will increase their son's sexual activity. The fact is that knowledge about sex doesn't make boys want to run out and have sex. Sexual knowledge is empowering. It helps boys feel secure and gives them the tools they need to make rational, reasonable decisions.

Don't worry that you might be telling your son too much. Children do not absorb any more than what they are ready to handle developmentally. Information that's out of their range of understanding and too sophisticated for their brains to comprehend will evaporate into thin air. This is true about all things, not just sex.

Do be concerned with how you present the material. Keep it as age appropriate as possible. Obviously, it wouldn't be appropriate to show a ten- or eleven-year-old explicit videos. If your four-year-old child asks, "Where do babies come from?," it isn't helpful to respond with information about fallopian tubes, follicle stimulating hormones, amniotic fluid, and the uterine environment. If you aren't sensitive to the developmental stage of your son, you're going to lose a teaching moment. Know where he is developmentally and answer the questions he asks *accurately* within his field of understanding.

Obstacle 2: Waiting for boys to ask questions

If you wait for your son to ask, it might be too late. Did he walk up to you one day and ask, "Will you teach me how to use a fork and spoon?" or "What's that big bowl in the bathroom with water in it that swirls all around sometimes?" Probably not. What you did in those cases was take the initiative. You looked for opportunities to teach about the fork and the spoon. You watched for chances to help your child learn about the toilet.

Do the same with sex. Look for opportunities to talk about sexuality. Don't wait to have "the talk." That's not how it's going to happen. Your son is not going to walk up to you and say, "I want to have the sex talk now." Remember, by the time *you* are ready to have "the talk," your son has already been talking and listening to lots of sex talk somewhere else.

The goal is to support your boys in becoming fabulous, wonderful, sexually complex men. This involves teaching them about taking care of and being responsible for their bodies by making healthy choices about nutrition, hygiene, teeth, hair, and skin. It also includes learning about gender, feelings, bodies, the nature of maleness and femaleness, relationships, love, intimacy, values, and communication. And it means giving them the facts.

Sexuality is one of many facets of the human personality and a fundamental building block of who we are, how we treat other people, and how we treat ourselves. Facts are important, but talking about the "facts of life" is not enough. Healthy sex education includes teaching values, communication skills, and decision-making skills. It involves learning to respect oneself and others in both body and spirit. Sex education is about shaping an entire way of experiencing life.

The method I am advocating is to take the best of your parenting skills and experiences and apply them to sex, rather than making a separate, special category and time for sexual discussions.

Obstacle 3: Believing that your son doesn't want or need education about sex and sexuality

We are sexual beings. Sexuality is part of every aspect of our lives. Look at the world in which we live. Popular music has sexual overtones. Magazines have pictures of women and men with little or no clothing. Television shows are full of sexual references and moments of casual sex.

Whether he thinks he needs it or not, your son will receive sex education. If you don't provide it, the world around him will do it for you. Who do you prefer takes on that role?

Obstacle 4: Not knowing what to say

You don't have to be a sex expert to teach about sex. You are not a dentist; yet you teach your son to brush and care for his teeth. You are not a doctor; still, you teach your son how to take care of himself when he has a cold or is feeling sick. You are not a grammar teacher; yet you teach your son how to use words and the appropriate order to use to create sentences.

You don't need to know everything. Stick to the basics of what you do understand. Keep yourself informed as best you can.

Obstacle 5: Embarrassment. Believing that polite people don't discuss sex

It has been said that it is easier to *do* sex than to *talk* about sex. Please remember, if you are embarrassed talking about sex, embarrassment is *your* issue and *your* problem, not your son's. Apprehensiveness is something your child will sense from your demeanor and attitude. Your embarrassment may prompt uneasiness in your son and a resistance to approaching you with questions about sex.

If you have had a traumatic sexual experience, an unfulfilled sexual relationship, or have experienced sexual identity confusion, you may not be ready to talk about sexual issues. Let your son know that his sexual questions are important to you and that you will help him by getting someone who can talk to him about his concerns. Get someone you can trust, a family member, close friend, or trusted therapist is appropriate.

Obstacle 6: Not wanting your son to ask you about your own sex life

Sooner or later your son will ask an embarrassing question in his search for more information and understanding. Get ready. The questions will come.

"Do you have sex?"

"Do you like sex?"

"How often do you do it?"

"Did you do it before you met Mom?"

"Did you do it before you had me?"

"If you don't want to have more kids, why do you still do it?"

You don't have to answer questions you aren't comfortable answering. An important lesson for boys to learn is that social norms exist around asking questions of a personal nature. Personal privacy needs to be respected.

Here are suggested responses to some of those questions that are too personal for your comfort level.

"I'm uncomfortable with answering that question completely for you right now, but I will tell you…"

"I don't want to influence your decisions about sex by telling you what I did or didn't do."

"How would having that information help you with the choices and decisions you're making about sex?"

"That question is personal and private. Couples don't usually talk about their personal sex lives with others."

Don't leave the sexual education of your son in the hands of the school, television, or his peer group. Seize the teaching moments he makes available to you. Work on overcoming the obstacles that are stopping you from reclaiming your role as his primary sex educator. Begin today.

Guidance in Getting Started

It's at this point that many parents need guidance. They don't want their boys to get their information about sexuality from acquaintances on the street. They would rather that information comes from them, but they aren't quite sure how to go about beginning the process. The seven points below will assist you in taking the first steps in teaching sex and sexuality in your home.

Point #1: Foster healthy attitudes.

Learning about sexuality is a lifelong process that begins at birth. A baby's attitudes about sexuality begin to form based on how they are held or touched. As children grow, they learn from watching their parents. They observe how they show affection, act around people of the same and different gender, and respond to nudity. They also form attitudes about sexuality through their exposure to TV, movies, music, books and magazines, and the Internet. Unfortunately, many myths about sexuality are perpetuated by the media and entertainment business. To counteract these influences, it is critical for parents to foster healthy attitudes toward sex by creating a home atmosphere in which sexual issues can be comfortably raised and discussed.

Point #2: Listen before you talk.

Adolescents and teenagers often claim to know everything about sex and aren't interested in what *you* have to say on the topic. If this occurs, switch gears and engage them in a discussion about what *they* know. Ask them to shed light on the topic for you from a teenage perspective. Use the phrases below to help you lead into a listening discussion:

"Tell me what you know so far."

"What have you been hearing?"

"What do your friends tell you about that?"

"What parts are you sure of?"

"How would you answer a friend who asked about that?"

Once they begin talking, you will glean valuable information on what they do and don't know about the topic. You may then be able to correct misinformation without seeming to lecture or to force your opinion on them. If nothing else, by asking for information you have begun a dialogue and kept the lines of communication open for future discussion.

Be willing to listen to your son and demonstrate that willingness by refusing to lecture and give information too quickly. You are on a fact-finding mission here. You will collect no facts if you do all the talking.

If your eight-year-old son asks you what a condom is, start by asking him what he knows about condoms and what specific information he would like to have. This will give you a reference point from which to provide more information. At eight, he probably doesn't need pictures or a demonstration. A simple explanation of the purpose and importance of using a condom will probably be enough. Let him know that when he wants more information all he needs to do is ask, just like he did this time.

Point #3: Avoid lecturing.

Do you want your point to be heard? You have a minute or less to get your message across before your son's emotional system kicks in and prevents him from hearing you. When you begin to drone on or start a lecture, a static noise will arise in his mind and drown out what you're saying, and he'll begin to tune you out.

Some teachable moments will arise spontaneously; others you will be able to plan ahead of time to craft more precisely the message you want to convey. Either way, you still have less than a minute to get your point across.

While the initial message is delivered in only a minute, the remainder of the discussion may take as long as your son needs it to last. Your parenting responsibility is to allow him to share his feelings, ask clarifying questions, or offer an opinion. He might have nothing further to ask or add. That's okay. You just planted a seed. Let it grow. More opportunities will arise for you to provide additional information.

Point #4: Be honest with your answers.

If a child asks about sex, it's usually an indication that he's been thinking about it and is in need of and ready for more information. Your son will quickly learn whether he can or can't trust the accuracy of your answers. If he feels he can't trust you, he'll stop asking you his important sexual questions and turn elsewhere for answers.

If your nine-year-old son wants to know what a "blow job" is, begin by asking him a few questions of your own to clarify his question so you can be more accurate in your response.

"What do you already know about blow jobs?"

"Were you talking about them at school with some of your friends?"

"Where did you hear about blow jobs?"

Avoid asking, "Why do you want to know that?" or saying, "Kids your age don't need to know about those things. Those are terrible words to say. Don't talk like that around here," or "Don't let your mother hear you talk that way."

Give him accurate information without chastising him for asking the question. Explain what a blow job is and that it is a part of having sex. For some people, oral sex is only part of what they do for others in the beginning part called foreplay.

Discuss appropriate times, places, and people to have oral sex with. This is the time to talk about your own feelings about oral sex and clarify your personal moral position. Remember, many adolescents and teens don't consider a "blow job" to be a sexual act. Be sure your child understands that it *is* an act of sex and that sexually transmitted infections can be acquired this way.

Point #5: Recognize teaching moments.

Stay open to the teachable moments that regularly present themselves. Those opportunities abound, and you will find them if you look for them purposefully.

You can create many teachable moments by keeping a close eye on the news. Children are aware of what is happening in the news. They hear about it at school, on TV or the radio, talking to their peers, and overhearing your conversations. Use that information. Read the Internet article that caught their attention at the dinner table. Begin a discussion. Share opinions.

Notice billboards on the roadside, posters in the mall, and commercials on television. Use what your boys are being exposed to and help them better understand the world in which they live. Debrief what is going on. Explain the hidden messages. Point out the sexual overtones. Correct any myths about sexuality. Confront social injustices. Interpret the event. Provide alternative points of view.

When your toddler is touching his penis, you have a teachable moment where you can talk about accurate names of body parts or appropriate times and places to touch yourself. When your third grader mentions gym class and how boys are better in sports than girls, you have a teachable moment where you can talk about gender stereotyping. When your adolescent is considering going to the sixth-grade dance, you have a teachable moment where you can talk about respecting other people's bodies. When your teenage son starts getting regular texts from girls, you have a teachable moment where you can talk about love and relationships. Teachable moments are everywhere and happen regularly. These moments are your opportunity to provide brief information about sexuality.

Point #6: Use accurate terminology.

"Keep little Willy in your pants."

"Aim your pecker in the middle of the toilet."

"Don't touch her boobs."

"The ball hit him right in the family jewels."

Please use phrases that reflect accurate terminology for body parts. Call a penis a penis, not a Willy, a worm, or any other slang term you perceive as cute. Breasts are breasts, not boobs, knockers or titties. Testicles are testicles, not balls, nuts, or family jewels.

Boys need to know what the body parts are called, how they work, and gender differences. Don't confuse the matter by making up cute words to replace anatomical terms. Let go of your anxiety about saying the correct word and get on with being the primary sex educator of your son at an early age.

Point #7: Provide age-appropriate information.

When giving information about where babies come from, it's important to know where your child is developmentally and provide them information within their field of understanding. If your four-year-old asks, "Where do babies come from?" and you respond by saying,

"Okay, you've got your fallopian tubes and some follicle-stimulating hormone, some amniotic fluid, and a uterine environment..." you're going to lose a valuable teaching moment. Give sexual information appropriate to your child's developmental level.

If your three-year-old wants to know what's in your tampon box, don't overreact. Remember, this is a three-year-old asking the question.

To an adult, the question is about a box containing an object that is placed inside a sexual organ and therefore has something to do with sex. To the child, it's a question about a box and nothing more. Answer as if you were answering a question about a box of tissues. Say something like, "It contains a soft piece of tissue that women use" or "It's a little box that adults use to put stuff in."

If your ten-year-old son wants to know what's inside a tampon box, it's still a question about a box, and it's a great opportunity to begin educating him about women's bodies and their menstrual cycles. Keep the information brief. Don't deliver a lecture that makes him hesitate before asking more questions.

__Important Myths about Sex to Dispel__

Boys of all ages are full of misinformation and untruths about sexual issues. Many myths abound and need to be corrected in order for boys to become men who live sexual lives based on fact rather than on ideas and opinions that may be faulty.

The following section is a reference guide to help you address some of the myths that currently exist about sex. When you see these myths on TV, hear your son verbalize one, or notice behavior based on a myth, confront it.

Myth #1: Women want to be talked into having sex.

This is an extremely popular notion in the media. Be aware that this myth is being perpetrated regularly in movies, TV, and books. The woman says no two or three times, and the man keeps pushing or asking. Eventually, she falls passionately into his arms. She has defended her honor enough and is now free to say yes and submit to the man's plea.

If you have not talked about and dispelled this myth with your son, he's learning that when a woman says yes it means yes. When she says no it means keep asking and eventually you'll get what you want. He's being taught that all he has to do is pay for dinner and a movie, ask endlessly, and eventually he'll get what he wants. Basically, he simply has to outlast the girl.

This is not a message we want our boys, or our girls, to grow up believing. If you have not yet had this discussion with your son, do it tonight.

Myth #2: If a woman wants sex, she must be a slut.

Women are not sluts, whores, prostitutes, or sex addicts because they like sex. Women are beautiful, fabulous sexual beings who enjoy the pleasure of sharing a sexual experience with their partner. They are no better or worse than men who enjoy the same sexual experiences.

The sexual behavior of both men and women is pretty similar. It's how that behavior is reported that's dissimilar. The difference is due primarily to the level of social acceptance granted to each gender.

Men are more likely to boast of their sexual exploits, while women tend to downplay their sexual experiences. Women are frowned upon for talking about sex, especially when they say they want or like it. Clearly, a double standard exists where sexual acceptance is concerned.

Refrain from using language that perpetuates this double standard.

"Nice girls don't find sex all that much fun."

"Women just do it to please their husbands or to have children."

"Men are real animals in the bedroom."

"Just fake that you like it."

"It's the man's job to initiate sex."

Be careful how you talk about sex and sex roles with your son. You may be planting seeds of belief that bear the fruit of toxic masculinity.

Myth #3: Jealousy is an expression of love.

Jealous people have a strong need to control the object of their affection. They often believe they need and deserve the full attention of that person and feel lost, lonely, and frightened when the person is not solely focused on them. They feel diminished if their "loved one" shows attention to someone or something else.

Jealousy is a way an unloving person attempts to get what they want: attention and being taken care of. They often become angry and sometimes violent if they don't get what they want. Do not mistake this for love.

There are two types of love. Jealousy is not one of them. The two basic types are *eros*: erotic or sexual love; and *agape*: selfless or spiritual love.

Look for opportunities to point out how love is present in your son's life. Demonstrate and articulate the many ways real love is expressed in your family and among your social groups.

Myth #4: Homosexuality is abnormal.

Left-handed people are not more emotionally disturbed than right-handed people. Although being right-handed occurs more frequently, one is not better than the other. One is not right and the other wrong. Right-handed, left-handed, or ambidextrous, a person is simply who they are.

The same is true about sexuality. There is no scientific evidence in the fields of psychiatry or psychology that homosexuality is any more of an emotional or personality dysfunction than heterosexuality.

Myth #5: Homosexuals have a greater likelihood of seducing young children.

This is fabricated information based solely on fear and ignorance. The fact is that over 90 percent of cases of sexual abuse occur between a heterosexual man and a girl. End of story.

__Topics to Confront Directly__

Topic #1: Examples of Gender Stereotyping

"You throw like a girl."

"A woman's place is in the home."

"Asians are terrible drivers."

"Big boys don't cry."

"Women are so emotional."

"White men can't jump."

"Boys are better at sports."

"Gay men are weak and effeminate."

"Mowing the grass is a man's job."

These statements and others like them perpetuate myths and provide inaccurate information about gender and race. Men cry, cook, and clean the house, and it has nothing to do with their being gay or straight. Women run businesses, fight in the army, and mow the grass because that is part of who they are and how they choose to be.

The messages that you as a parent communicate concerning tolerance and acceptance are subtle, yet extremely powerful. They shape how boys see the world and the people in it. Your son is learning a great deal about sexuality by what you say to him that reflects a gender bias or an acceptance of diverse sexualities and genders, such as lesbian, gay, bisexual, transgender, queer, or asexual. Through your words, he learns about bigotry and prejudice or about love and grace. How you talk to your son about the world in which he lives and the people he encounters in it influences his view and affects his experiences.

Be mindful of the words you use and the message you want to impart. Take every opportunity to confront gender stereotyping language that perpetuates a misleading and unhealthy perception of self and others.

Topic #2: Confronting sexual and racial stereotyping

Language that confronts sexual and racial stereotyping:

"That's sexual stereotyping."

"That's sexual harassment."

"That's racist."

"That sounds like stereotyping to me."

"Words like that are hurtful."

"When you say that, you're demonstrating intolerance."

Boys often use language that needs to be confronted directly. They make statements like, "That's so gay," or "You're such a fag." They hear it in school and use the language among their peers. They laugh at others who aren't like them and call each other names that reinforce misconceptions about gender, race, and sexuality. When this happens, a parent, or any other adult present, needs to step in and correct the language misuse.

Labeling a certain type of behavior "gay" or calling someone a "dyke" or "lesbo" is far more than just name-calling. Boys need to know what their words mean and the effect those words have on others and the world around them. If parents don't correct a boy's misperceptions and language patterns, the stereotype is reinforced and the myth about gender identity remains a constant in our society.

A carefully crafted lecture is not necessary when you hear stereotyping language. Keep your comments brief and to the point. Say,

"That's sexual stereotyping," to draw attention to your son's statement. Follow that initial statement with a *because statement* that provides additional information.

"That's racist *because* the color of a person's skin has nothing to do with their abilities."

"That's sexual stereotyping *because* boys and girls act in a variety of ways, regardless of their gender preference."

"That's sexual harassment *because* you're using your maleness to influence that girl's decisions."

"That's hurtful *because* you're making an assumption about that person's character."

When parents ignore their son's inappropriate statements, he is left with the impression that it's okay to say such things and that it's accurate. It's not okay, and it is the parents' responsibility to confront their boys when sexual stereotyping takes place.

Topic #3: Confronting catcalling

The way a woman dresses is the way she chooses to dress. Her choice is based on her comfort level, style preference, or clothing functionality. Allowing boys or men to call out sexually suggestive comments to a woman is allowing sexual harassment. When you hear it happening, confront the catcaller immediately. "It's not okay to talk to people like that," or "That's harassment. In our family we don't talk to women like that."

My wife Valerie is a triathlete. She has competed on the state and national levels, taking first place overall in dozens of races and first in her age group countless times. We live in Michigan, which means she spends hours in the pool swimming. She has tried several swimsuit styles and has picked the one she thinks is best for her training. It's sleek and form fitting. When she walks across the pool complex to the lap swim section, she is not strutting around looking for someone to have sex with. She is not thinking about hooking up with someone. She's thinking about her training routine and preparing for the next race. To suggest that she dresses the way she does to get attention is insulting. To shout out to her, "Oh baby, you look hot," or any other sexually suggestive comment, is not about her and what she's wearing. It's about what is going on in the mind of the person doing the shouting. To ask her to take responsibility for someone else's inappropriate behavior by putting on a loose, baggy swimsuit is ridiculous and degrading. Deal with the shouter. That's where the problem lies.

Topic #4: Confronting "should" statements

A "should have" statement is designed to impose guilt. Its intent is to shame and blame. "Should have" statements are verbal attempts to manipulate someone into doing what you want them to do. The underlying message is *I'm right, you're wrong.* Further, *I'm better than you.*

"You should have listened to me."

"She should be on time."

"You should have minded your own business."

"You should have called him right away."

"You should have told me sooner."

"They shouldn't say those kinds of things."

"You should have asked me."

"You should have paid closer attention."

"He should be more courteous."

"You should have saved the money."

"You should have thought of that earlier."

When boys "should on" others, they create models in their heads of how the world "should be." Then, when others don't live up to their expectations, they create emotions of anger, irritation, and frustration. They believe others should be different, and they become intolerant, not accepting what is in the here-and-now of life.

Confront "should" language whenever you hear your son using it. Help him accept people as they are and not expect others to be what and how he wants them to be. People are what they are. The world is what it is.

Topic #5: Confronting jokes and rape talk

Confront the use of dirty jokes, dumb blonde jokes, racial jokes, and rape talk in your home. Allowing this kind of talk sends the message to boys that it's okay to stereotype others and make fun of their differences as long as it gets a laugh. Jokes about the shortcomings of others promote a "better than" mentality. They're an attempt to build oneself up through the process of tearing another down. They are the breeding ground of intolerance. Let's find a person who is different from us, embellish that difference, sprinkle a little humor on it, and laugh together about it. Later, that joke has grown into a belief that affects the way those who laughed at it see and treat others.

Rape talk is using the word rape in a nonsexual context. Examples: "Did you see the football game last night? Our team got totally raped." "I got raped by new security standards at work today." "That last exam really raped my grade point." When we use the word in such a trivial way it negates the harsh reality of sexual rape in our culture and the devastating effects it has on the lives of so many women—and men, as well. The word should not be used in any other context than that of sexual assault. When it is, confront it immediately.

Teaching Boundary Setting

An easy way to understand boundaries is to think about your bottom line. What will or won't you do or allow? A boundary is something you establish *for yourself.* You can't establish a boundary for someone else. Physical boundaries involve physical closeness, touch, and intimacy. Emotional boundaries protect us from feelings of blame, shame, and ridicule that others may try to impose upon us.

It's important to recognize that boundaries are learned. If as a child your personal boundaries weren't valued, chances are you didn't learn how to establish your bottom line and stand up for what you will and won't allow.

Dysfunctional families use boundaries to punish, intimidate, and control. Those in authority impose rigid rules and regulations on the children and leave no room for individual choices and decision making.

Chaotic families exercise no boundaries, invading a child's emotional, physical, and mental spaces. The child's wants, needs, and rights are ignored. When children don't feel safe or cared for as individuals, they don't develop a solid sense of their own identity.

Healthy families create and maintain boundaries that help each member feel their own identity is safe in the world. Boundaries help children set limits so they can be in healthy relationships that enrich, support, and inspire them.

Teach your son to make boundaries that are clear, specific, and positive. "Remember to keep your hands to yourself unless you ask for and receive permission" focuses on what you do want rather than on what you don't want and makes the boundary clear. "No touching without permission" creates a clear boundary but focuses on what you don't want. Stick to the positive phrasing.

Make personal boundary setting in your family each individual's privilege and responsibility. Yes, that includes the children. Any type of touch can be a violation when the one being touched doesn't want it. Whatever the situation, the most appropriate person to decide when and if their personal space is being invaded is the one being touched. Allow the person who is on the receiving end to decide what is too much or too close. "I didn't poke him that hard" or "It didn't hurt" are not acceptable excuses from the perpetrator when someone is touched who did not want to be touched. Such excuses assume that the level of hurt inflicted determines whether a boundary has been violated. It does not. When your daughter's first boyfriend touches her breast softly in the car on the way home, the fact that it "doesn't hurt" isn't the criterion you want to use in deciding what is "appropriate" touching.

When you notice that your son has crossed a boundary, confront it directly by saying, "Jason that is space invading. We don't do that without someone's permission because people deserve to define and control their own space. What we do here is ask, 'Do you mind if I give you a hug,' or 'Can I rub your sore arm?'"

10 Behaviors That Create Boundary Confusion

1. Teasing, putdowns and name-calling are boundary violations, but many parents let it happen under the guise, "Oh, I was just joking around."

2. Removing a child's bedroom door is a boundary violation. It's taking away a person's sense of privacy and personal space just because the parent didn't like the behavior of slamming a door in anger.

3. Tickling a child until they can barely breathe and ignoring their pleas to stop teaches them that their request to have a boundary respected can be violated by someone bigger and stronger. They become less likely to respect the pleas of another when they are in a position of strength or power.

4. Not knocking on bedroom and bathroom doors before entering teaches children there is no need to respect the privacy of others.

5. Forcing a child to share a toy when they're not ready to give it up teaches the child to give to someone what they want when the other wants it, even if the child is not ready to relinquish their turn. The underlying message is: share even if you don't want to. When asked to share, allow children to finish their turn and give what is requested to the other person when and if they're ready.

6. Using "please" as a magic word that requires others to comply, regardless of whether they want to or not. In our attempt to teach manners to children, we give the word

please a lot of power. "Say the magic word and you can have a piece of candy." "Say *please* first." "You can't have that until you say *please*." It's important to teach children manners, and they also need to be taught that just because you said *please* doesn't guarantee you're going to get what you want. Don't let *please* go beyond its polite usage and take on the power to persuade.

7. Kissing without permission is a boundary violation. Allowing Grandma or Aunt Tilly to give a child a big wet kiss when they didn't want one is how we teach kids to give a person in authority what they want, when they want it. Down goes the boundary.

8. Hugging without permission is also a boundary violation. Your son does not have to be hugged if he doesn't want a hug. Even gentle touches are not okay if the child doesn't feel like being touched. Help boys learn to say, "I don't really want a hug right now," or "I'm not comfortable being kissed."

9. Being taught to please others. Do you have difficulty saying no? Difficulty saying no comes from a child being taught to please others even when it means going beyond their own comfort level. As an adult they feel terrible about themselves when they don't do what others want. Their need to please goes unfulfilled.

10. Making demands without opportunities for choice. Do you expect your son to do it NOW just because you say so? Or does he have some choice around when and how he does it? The more choice he has, the more personal power he

has. He may say, "Can I do it in five minutes after I finish this?"

Teaching Boys How to Speak Up for Themselves

Teach boys to speak up for themselves appropriately. If you want a behavior, you have to teach a behavior. When boys learn the appropriate way to speak up for themselves, they are more likely to hear effectively and respond empathetically when a girl speaks up for herself.

Two important teaching pieces are necessary here.

First, teach boys to give a directive.

"Please step back."

"I want more space."

"Please stop poking me."

Second, teach boys to precede or follow a directive with information about why they want what they've asked for. The information that follows a directive begins with the word "because."

"Please step back *because* I'm uncomfortable with your being this close. You're in my space."

"I want more space *because* I need room to do this activity."

"Please stop poking me *because* it interrupts my reading and I want to finish this chapter." The "why" can be delivered before the directive. "Poking interrupts my reading and prevents me from finishing this chapter. Please stop poking me" is as helpful as the first form." Either is fine.

Teaching Self-Questioning

Teaching children to ask questions of themselves as they contemplate sex will help them make their sexual choices from a conscious rather than an unconscious space. When they learn the technique of self-questioning, they learn to explore wants, needs, and possible outcomes from a position of personal power. They take control of a situation and lessen the chance they will say later, "It just happened," or "I just got carried away."

Questions young people should ask themselves as they contemplate sex or drugs include:

- Do I feel comfortable?
- Do I feel pressured?
- How do I want to feel?
- Could I get hurt by this?
- Is this the type of person I want to be?
- How would I feel if a friend was doing this?
- Is this the type of relationship I want to have with my girlfriend/boyfriend?
- What is my purpose for wanting to do this?
- What do I hope to accomplish by having sex now?
- Will this be an enjoyable experience for me?
- How will I feel about it tomorrow?
- Would there be a better time/place to do this?
- Am I prepared to accept the consequences?
- Does my rational mind agree with my hormones?

Self-questioning is a technique that can be applied to many situations in a child's life. When you teach your boys to self-question, you're teaching them a process they can use in any new or uncertain situation. You are teaching them to check it out inside and listen to their inner voice, a valuable life skill they can use for years to come.

Life Examples

"My roommates are heading for trouble," Micah informed his parents on his first weekend home from college.

"What do you mean?" his father asked.

"They're wild. They stay out all night, drink, and skip classes. One of them has had sex with three different girls that I know of."

"Must have had really permissive parents," Micah's mother said.

"No. Just the opposite," Micah responded. "They both come from families where they were highly controlled. It's like they've never had a chance to try anything, so they're doing everything all at once. Now that the person who controlled them isn't around, they don't know how to control themselves. Their accelerators are working, but they don't know how to use their brakes."

"That's too bad," Micah's father said.

"Yes, it is," Micah agreed. "I certainly am grateful you allowed me to make some mistakes growing up. Thanks for encouraging me to trust my own judgment even at those times when I didn't appear too smart."

"You're welcome," both parents said in unison.

*****

Claude was sliding the last batch of muffins into the oven when his nine-year-old son Ricky interrupted with a question. "Dad, why are people gay?"

Claude closed the oven door and said, "Let's go sit in the other room for a few minutes and we can talk about your question." As Claude walked slowly with his son into the living room, he began constructing a response. He knew he had to keep it short and to the point.

The two sat down on the couch together. Claude began by asking, "Ricky, what got you thinking about this topic?"

"Well, there's a new kid at school and I heard him tell Eric at lunch that he has two dads," Ricky replied. "That just got me thinking. How do some people become gay?"

Claude took a slow, deep breath and said, "Well, people don't *become* gay, they just are who they are. Most people are right-handed, some are left-handed. That's just the way they are. The same is true about our attraction to people of the opposite sex or the same sex. Most people like someone of the opposite sex, others like someone of the same sex. If I'm right-handed I don't make someone wrong for being left-handed. That's just who they are. The important thing is that your new classmate has parents who love him and are there to care for him, regardless of whether they're right-handed or left-handed, gay or straight."

They both sat quietly for a moment as Ricky appeared to be processing what his dad just said. After about thirty seconds, he said, "Okay, I think I got it. Thanks."

"Anything else?" Claude asked.

"Nope, that's it."

"Let me know if you have any other questions. I think I'll go check on those muffins."

*****

Veronica was on her way to her bedroom to call it a night. As she walked past her seventeen-year-old son Pablo's room, she noticed the door was slightly open. Her son was sitting at his desk staring at the wall. She knocked lightly. "Hey, I'm heading to bed."

Pablo jumped. "Oh! You startled me. I was deep in thought."

"Sorry to startle you. What were you thinking about?" Veronica asked.

"My girlfriend. We've been dating for a year and a half, and…" Pablo paused and looked down at the floor.

"It's okay to talk to me about anything," Veronica assured her son. "That's been our agreement your entire life. Whatever it is, I won't judge you, and we'll figure it out together."

"Well, I've been thinking about having sex with Maria," Pablo said hesitantly. "But I don't know if I should. I don't want to upset her and lose her as a girlfriend."

"Thank you for sharing that with me, Pablo," Veronica replied. "I like it that you're asking yourself some questions before taking action. That demonstrates maturity." She paused and then asked, "Have you said anything to Maria about your thoughts of having sex?"

"It came up once, but it was kind of awkward, and we just stopped talking about it."

"It's important that you both trust your feelings and never pressure the other person to do something they're not comfortable doing," Veronica said.

"I know," Pablo replied, and then sat quietly.

Veronica waited a moment before asking, "Do you remember the time you had a sleepover at Matthew's house when he got in a big argument with his mother?"

"Yeah," Pablo replied.

"Think back to what it felt like when you were there and Matthew and his mother were screaming and yelling at each other and throwing things. You didn't like it. You were so uncomfortable that you called me and I came and picked you up. On the way home you said you never wanted to sleep over at his house again. Do you remember that feeling?"

"Yeah, I do."

Veronica continued, "That feeling was letting you know that something was off, and it wasn't right for you. It's probably a feeling similar to what you had when the topic of sex came up with Maria. For whatever reason, it just wasn't right. Trust and honor that feeling whenever it comes up."

"All right, I think I can do that," Pablo said.

"Just let yourself settle with that for now. We can talk more about this whenever you're ready. Good night, Pablo," Veronica said to her son as she turned and started walking out of the room.

"Thanks, Mom. Good night," Pablo called to her as she left.

*****

Sean attended a government camp for boys during the summer between eleventh and twelfth grades. The camp was being sponsored by a university near the state capital. Teenage boys came from across the state and stayed in campus dorms for an entire week. Although all the boys were the same age, they were a diverse group, representing a variety of ethnic, cultural, and economic backgrounds. It was sure to be an enriching experience for all involved, and Sean was looking forward to it.

Each day after lunch the boys were given ninety minutes of free time. Most of the two hundred plus boys remained in the cafeteria lounge to socialize. On the first day, a small group of girls passed by the window. The girls were attending a volleyball camp and were staying in a nearby dorm. As they walked by, several boys began shouting and whistling at them. The girls lowered their heads and hurried on. A few minutes later another group of girls walked past, and this time even more boys participated in the whistling and shouting. Sean began to have an uncomfortable feeling in his stomach as he noticed the girls' reaction to the boys' relentless calls. Uncertain about what to do, he quietly exited the cafeteria and returned to his dorm room.

After lunch on the second day, the same whistling and shouting occurred as the girls walked by. Sean noticed that this time twice as many guys participated. Again he retreated to his dorm room. As he lay on the bed staring at the ceiling, he could hear faint whistles and laughter coming from the cafeteria.

Sean decided that something needed to be done. Later that evening he talked to a camp counselor about what was going on during afternoon free time. The counselor smiled, shrugged his shoulders, and said, "Boys will be boys. If the girls don't like it, they should take a different route back to their dorm."

The catcalling scenario was repeated each day following lunch for the remainder of the week. Every day Sean would quickly eat his lunch and head straight back to his dorm room. In his mind, the end of the week couldn't come soon enough.

Saturday morning finally came, and Sean was up early waiting for his parents' arrival. When they came, he wasted no time signing out, loading his backpack in the trunk, and jumping into the back seat of the car.

Excited to hear about their son's week, Sean's mom didn't hesitate. As the car pulled away from the curb, she asked, "What was something interesting you learned from the week at camp?"

"I learned something, but I wouldn't call it interesting. It was bothersome," Sean responded, and he proceeded to tell his parents about the behavior displayed by the boys and his feelings about it. He related what he had said to the counselor and how he would hide out in his room every afternoon because he wasn't sure what else to do.

Sensing frustration in Sean's voice as he talked about the experience, his dad commented, "Sean, you learned several important lessons here. You learned to listen to your feelings and knew that what those boys were doing was wrong. You made a conscious choice to not participate in the harassment of the girls. You attempted to create change by talking to a person in charge and letting him know about the inappropriate behavior. You also took care of yourself by staying away from the behavior that bothered you. You did the right thing, even when others were not."

Sean and his parents spent the rest of the car ride home talking about all the other experiences Sean had during the week and what he learned from them.

<u>Conclusion</u>

Facts on how babies are made, how not to get pregnant, and how to protect oneself against sexually transmitted infections is a small part of the education boys need about sexuality. Indeed, your responsibility as a parent goes well beyond that of teaching facts about sex.

The goal of reclaiming your role as a sex educator is to support your son in becoming a fabulous, wonderful, sexual being. Sexuality is a facet of the human personality. It's a fundamental building block in structuring who your son is, how he treats himself, and how he treats other people.

Lesson 9: Teaching about Consent

Boys need to be taught what consent is and what it is not. This leaves parents in a bind when our society has misconstrued the definition of consent. In popular culture, when a boy hears no, he takes it as a challenge to keep pushing and prodding until he gets a yes. In teaching a more responsible definition to our boys, we must be thorough and diligent. It is a step-by-step process that must be repeated at each developmental level. Boys need to learn the concept of consent in kindergarten through second grade, again in third through fifth grades, then again in sixth through eighth grades, again in high school and, yes, again at age eighteen to twenty-one. With repeated learning, they are able to incorporate what consent really means into their manhood.

What Is Consent?

Consent is agreement to engage in an activity with another. It's saying yes to mutual participation in an activity. That activity could be having tea, watching a movie, jogging in the park, or having sexual contact. Consent is something that should always be given freely. A person who is forced, threatened, or badgered to give consent has done so under duress, and that consent is not valid. It is not consent if the person is afraid to say no. Furthermore, the person who gave consent to participate in an activity must be able to stop the activity at any point if they so choose. Are you willing to teach this definition of consent to your boys?

Teaching the Components of Consent

Consent requires these components:

1. Consent is a verbal agreement. How a person dresses, smiles, looks, or acts does not mean they want to have sex with you. Appearance, body language, or any other form of nonverbal communication should not be interpreted as consent.

2. Consent requires clear and concise communication about expectations. Many people engage in intimate interpersonal interactions believing they are not having sex. They don't consider kissing, fondling each other's genitals, or even oral sex as *sex*. Former president Bill Clinton was quick to point out, "I did not have sex with that woman." It is important to clarify how you feel and how your partner feels about the sexual situation before initiating or continuing the sexual activity.

3. Consent cannot be assumed by relationship. Being in a dating relationship does not mean that consent to have sex has been given. The same goes for marriage. Being in a

marital relationship doesn't mean that consent to engage in sexual activity has been given. Marital rape is as serious as any other form of sexual assault.

4. Consent is limited to a one-time event. Giving consent to engage in sexual activity at one time is not an automatic agreement to engage in sexual activity at a later date. Previous sexual engagement does not override the necessity for consent for sexual activity at a future time.

5. Consent includes the option to change one's mind or stop at any time. Giving consent at the beginning of a sexual encounter does not mean you have to continue to the bitter end. When you're engaged in a warm embrace and kissing lightly but don't feel like being touched under your shirt, you get to say, "I don't feel like doing that now. I'd like to just keep kissing or stop altogether." When you're in the middle of hot, passionate sexual intercourse and you don't feel like having your partner's finger in your anus, you get to say, "I don't like that. Please stop."

6. Consent involves open communication among all participants. A person who is silent, not actively resistant, or passive is not giving consent. Even when a person doesn't verbalize "no" or resist physically, they are not agreeing to sexual activity.

7. Consent requires the capacity to decide. Being incapacitated, as when using alcohol or drugs, negates a person's ability to give consent. Making the decision "under the influence" creates a situation where it becomes

impossible for them to fully and completely understand what it is they are giving consent to.

Teaching the Process for Acquiring Autonomy

Asking for and giving consent presume a person's autonomy. Consent can only be given by an independent, responsible individual. A person who is not independent and self-directed is under someone else's direction and guidance. They don't have the power to give consent; the person doing the directing and guiding has the power. For a boy to become a man who honors and respects consent, he must learn to become an autonomous person. Boys who grow up in controlling environments where their autonomy isn't respected have difficulty both seeking consent and giving it.

Boys can learn how to be autonomous through a three-step process. You, as a parent, are going to have to teach them each step in that process. Are you ready for that task? It's not enough just to develop independent boys. The goal is to help boys become respectful and responsible autonomous people. The process outlined below is designed to help boys grow into responsible, empathetic, and self-reliant men who understand consent.

1. Through verbal responsibility
2. Through opportunities
3. Through choices

Step 1: How to teach verbal responsibility

The goal is to encourage boys to create their own voice: to speak up for themselves so they become independent, self-responsible individuals. Verbal responsibility, being responsible with the words we use, leads to responsible behavior. Our words structure and give meaning to our thoughts. Repetitive thoughts turn into beliefs. Beliefs influence our behaviors. It all begins with words. Words are the primary building blocks of our reality. A valuable resource on this topic is my book coauthored with Chick Moorman called *The Abracadabra Effect: The 13 Verbally Transmitted Diseases and How to Cure Them*.

To help boys become responsible and autonomous, we can expand on the concepts presented earlier in Lesson 4: Self-Responsible Language by teaching them how and when to speak up. Most boys don't know the appropriate times to interrupt, nor do they have the skills they need to do it effectively. They don't understand the power of words and how to use words to create change in their lives. Learning when and how to speak up helps boys grow in their understanding of consent.

Below are suggestions for when to encourage your son to speak up and examples of what he might say when he does. Boys need to speak up when:

1. They don't understand something.

Boys can become frustrated as they try to comprehend the mysteries of the world around them. It's hard for them to understand why things work the way they do. The more clarification they get from adults, the better able they are to grasp the abstract nature of their world. As parents, we need to be available and open for questions of any nature.

Teach your son to say, "I don't understand this. Can you help me figure it out?" "Will you explain this to me?"

2. They need help.

Boys need help stacking blocks, reaching toys on a high shelf, writing a thank-you letter, understanding a math concept, handling a peer relationship, and in many other situations as they move through each developmental stage. Some situations they can handle themselves. Others they cannot. A key component to becoming independent is knowing when and how to ask for help.

For some boys, whining becomes the preferred way of asking for help. Your parental role here is to give your son useful words to say instead of whining. By teaching him to say, "I want to stay up longer," "I want to be held," or "I want to get down," you help him learn that using words is his best hope for getting what he wants in your family. He also learns that whining doesn't work with you.

Say, "Brandon, that's whining. Whining doesn't work with me because I can't understand what you're saying and what you really want. Use your words to tell me what you want. By using words, you sometimes get what you want. Sometimes you don't. And it's your only hope."

3. They want something.

Wanting something and needing something are two different things. It's okay for boys to ask for what they need. It's also okay for them to use their voice to ask for what they want.

Just because a child learns to speak up and ask for what he wants doesn't mean he will get it. Some wants are unhealthy or unsafe. It's your job as a parent to deny those requests while respecting your son's right to voice his desire to have it.

Sometimes getting what you want is a matter of timing. Wanting a cookie is fine, and you might not get it until after dinner. It's permitted to want and even ask for a toy in the toy store. The toy may not be forthcoming until you create and implement a plan for how to get it. Say, "I hear how much you want that toy. What are you willing to do to help get it? What is your plan for paying for it?"

4. Their personal space has been violated.

Boys need to be taught to find and access their voice whenever they experience inappropriate touch. Teach your son to speak up clearly if he's touched inappropriately. Teach him to say, "That's not appropriate," or "Nobody gets to touch me there." Teach him to use his voice to tell you if anyone touches him in an inappropriate way, using words like "Dad, Billy touched me" or "I got a wrong touch."

Help your teen learn to say, "It's my body and I want you to respect it," and "The answer is no, and I don't need a reason."

When boys are taught to speak up when their own personal space is violated, they also learn to hear and respect the words of another when they speak up in defense of their personal space.

5. They have an idea.

Boys are great thinkers, especially if you encourage their thinking. They see the world from a different point of view than adults do. Their ideas are just as important to them as your ideas are to you. Allowing your son the opportunity to share his ideas and encouraging him to do so empowers him, stimulates his imagination, and encourages ownership of the results his ideas produce.

6. They have solutions to problems.

Encourage your son to speak up and offer possible solutions when problems arise. Involve him in solution-seeking meetings. Invite him to join in the brainstorming of possible solutions. Include his input as you attempt to reach consensus on a workable solution. There is always more than one way to solve a problem. Your son's solution may actually be the one that works best for him. By taking his suggestions seriously you encourage his thinking, help him see himself as a problem solver, and increase the chance that he will offer solutions in the future.

7. They have an opinion.

Boys have opinions. They care what you name the dog. It matters to them whether you paint their room blue or green. Where you go on your next family vacation is important to them.

We teach boys to use their voice to express opinions when we actively seek those opinions. It's important that you ask your son about his preferences. "What do you think about that?" "Do you have a different thought about that?" "What's your opinion?"

The belief that "my opinion counts" is a vital component in building self-esteem and self-confidence. By seeking boys' opinions and taking those opinions seriously, we help them to view themselves as capable, responsible, valuable human beings. When boys experience having their opinions matter at a young age, they learn to be more open to the opinions of others at an older age. They learn they can be both opinionated *and* receptive to the opinions of others.

8. They are asked a direct question.

Recently I asked a four-year-old how he was doing. The mother spoke for the child and replied, "He's feeling kind of shy today." The child never looked up. There was no need. The mother was his voice.

When you speak for your child, you teach him there is no need to use his own voice. You communicate that adults will do his thinking and talking for him. The message you send is, "Your voice is not important. There is no need to use it. I'll take care of all your thinking and responding." When you speak for your child, you encourage him to do less speaking for himself in the future.

9. Someone is in danger.

Whenever there is potential danger, we want and need boys to speak up, and we want them to do it quickly.

"I don't want to hear any tattling," a parent recently told her son as he began to tell a story about his older sister. But what if the older sister was stuck in a tree and was hanging from her broken ankle? What if the sibling was playing with matches? What if a schoolmate was urging her to sniff cleaning fluid?

Teach your son the difference between getting someone IN trouble and getting them OUT of trouble. If your son wants to tell you about how his sister took his ball so he can get her in trouble, teach him to use his voice to communicate what he wants and how he feels to his sister. Teach him to say, "I don't like it when you take my ball. I want you to give it back." Be there with him when he speaks to his sister to make sure his words are heard.

If you son witnesses a dangerous situation, teach him to communicate it quickly and directly. Give him some starter words that will tip you off that danger is involved. "Mom, I see danger," "Shannon needs help," or "trouble alert" work well as clues that danger is lurking.

10. They feel afraid, angry, sad, hurt or frustrated.

Teach your boys to communicate their feelings. Use feeling words in their presence often so they develop a broad-based feeling vocabulary. Say, "I'm feeling really angry right now," "I'm worried about my drive to work this morning because the snow is really piling up out there," or "I'm disappointed that I can't go for a bike ride because of the rain." By using feeling words yourself, you help your son learn about his own feelings and the need to express them. You give him permission to have feelings and teach him the names for those feelings so he is more likely to articulate them in the future.

Tell your youngster, "Seems like you're really angry with your brother right now. Why not tell him how angry you get when he marks on your paper?" Say to your teen, "Sounds to me like you're disappointed your dad wasn't there on time. It might be helpful to both of you if you communicate that to him."

When your child does share his fear, anger, or any other emotion, acknowledge it. Say, "Thank you for telling me, Andy. Will you say some more about it?" By not overreacting to his emotion you give him permission to acknowledge his feelings and work through them more quickly. You teach him the importance of sharing feelings and the value in listening to the feelings of others.

Step 2: How to teach about opportunities

Having life experiences is vital to a child's development. Opportunities provide the chance to experience life and learn from the lessons life offers. Opportunities for experience are essential in learning how to be an independent, responsible individual. If boys are not given the opportunity to do things on their own and experience the effects of their choices, they are more likely to become men who do not accept responsibility for what shows up in their life.

Boys need lots of opportunities. They also need to understand that every opportunity is paired with responsibility. Opportunity and responsibility stand together, attached at the hip, and they cannot be separated. They are equals. When responsibility declines, so does opportunity. It is essential that boys learn this fact of life.

Here are examples of how to teach this lesson to your son at each stage of development.

Toddler:

"You have the opportunity to play in the sand with your friend today. Your responsibility is to keep the sand below the knees."

"You have the opportunity to play with your blocks. Your responsibility is to put your blocks back in the block basket before getting out another toy."

Five-Year-Old:

"You have the opportunity to play outside this afternoon. Your responsibility is to stay in the backyard."

"You have the opportunity to watch your favorite TV show tonight. Your responsibility is to turn the TV off as soon as your show is over."

Nine-Year-Old:

"You have the opportunity to ride your bike today. Your responsibility is to ride in the neighborhood, staying away from busy Michigan Avenue."

"You have an opportunity to have a friend sleep over this Saturday. Your responsibility is to go to bed at the agreed upon time, which we'll discuss when he arrives."

Pre-Teen:

"You have the opportunity to play video games this afternoon. Your responsibility is to turn off the video games at six o'clock, as we discussed and agreed earlier."

"You have the opportunity to go to your cousin's for the weekend. Your responsibility is to have your homework completed before you go."

Teen:

"You have the opportunity to go to your friends' bonfire party. Your responsibility is to avoid alcohol and be home by midnight."

"You have the opportunity to use the car tonight. Your responsibility is to have only one passenger in the car and have the car back in the driveway by midnight."

At every age, continue to offer more choices as your son matures and demonstrates the ability to handle each opportunity in a responsible manner.

Step 3: How to teach about choices

To help your son see himself as responsible for his own behavior, use the words *choose, pick,* and *decide* regularly. "You decide" is language that shares power and control. It builds respect and fosters autonomy within a family. Language of this type gives your son a sense of control and the opportunity to have a voice in decisions that affect him and sometimes the family.

Telling your son, "You choose," communicates, "I trust you. I turn it over to you. I accept your decision even before I know what it is." It tells him that you're willing to accept his answer or solution and will support him in that decision.

Using the words *pick, choose,* and *decide* puts responsibility on your son's shoulders. Repetition is the key. Regularly hearing these words from you helps him learn that the outcome of his choice is on him, not on something you are doing to him.

Ways to Use Choose, Pick, Decide

1. To create awareness

When you want to help your son see himself as responsible for his own behavior, feelings, and attitudes, use *choose, pick, decide* to create awareness of the choices he is already making. It sounds like this:

Toddler: "I see you <u>chose</u> to make a mess." "I noticed you <u>decided</u> to use a spoon."

Six-Year-Old:

"You obviously <u>chose</u> to play in the mud." "I see you <u>picked</u> a warm outfit to wear."

Pre-Teen:

"I noticed you <u>chose</u> not to repeat the gossip." "Looks like you <u>decided</u> to get some extra study time in tonight."

Teen:

"I appreciate your <u>choosing</u> to call when you knew you would be late." "I noticed you <u>chose</u> to not call when you were going to be late. Next time please make a different choice." "I see you've <u>decided</u> to sleep in a bit this morning."

2. As a permission-giving alternative

When your son asks you a question such as, "Can I go outside to play?" and the answer is yes, use the permission-giving alternative. Instead of saying yes, give him permission to decide for himself.

"Can I have a snack?" Your reply is, "You choose."

"Can I call Grandma?" Your reply is, "You decide."

"May I do this later?" Your reply is, "You pick."

"Can I try out for the baseball team?" Your reply is, "That's up to you."

Please remember to use this technique only when the answer is yes. If your answer is no, then don't use this technique. Simply say, "No," and provide a reason, "Supper will be ready in fifteen minutes," or "It's getting late. You can call Grandma in the morning."

3. To encourage appropriate choices

An effective method of redirecting behavior resulting from an inappropriate choice your son has made is to use the phrase, "Please make a different choice." This verbal skill has three steps:

- State the problem.
- Say, "Please make a different choice."
- Let your son decide what different choice to make.

When siblings are contemplating a fight, tell them, "You sound like you're heading toward a fight. Please make a different choice." When your son is not playing by the rules, say, "You're choosing to go out of turn. That spoils the game for everyone. Please make a different choice."

"That loud voice is distracting to me. Please make a different choice" is a respectful way to communicate your discomfort with the noise level.

4. To make a cause-and-effect connection

Remember the Dynamic Discipline Equation? This is the four-step process involved.

Step 1: Explain the opportunity.

Step 2: Allow your son to choose.

Step 3: Follow through with the outcome.

Step 4: Give other opportunities.

For a refresher see Lesson 2: Teaching a Culture of Accountability.

Here's the process in practice.

Present the choice. "You can choose to pick up your toys or you can choose to leave them here. If you choose to pick them up, you will have decided to use them for the next week. If you decide to leave them here, I will pick them up, and you will have decided not to have them available for a week. You decide." The child makes the decision. He may choose to pick up his toys, and he may choose to leave them there.

The three words *choose, pick, decide* become the cornerstone of your family discipline policy.

With young boys, limit the choices.

- "You can choose the red cup or the blue cup. You decide."
- "You can decide to brush your teeth before story time or after. It's up to you."
- "You can choose to ride your tricycle or your scooter. You pick."

As they get older, begin to attach a related outcome to their choice.

- "If you choose to leave your toys in the middle of the living room, you'll be choosing to have them put on the shelf for a week."
- "If you choose to play quietly, you've decided to stay here with me in the kitchen."
- "When you choose to bring the car back with an empty gas tank, you've decided not to use the car next weekend."
- "If you choose to have all your chores completed by one o'clock, you can pick going to the mall for the rest of the afternoon."
- "If you choose to be in chat rooms on the computer, you will be deciding not to use the computer for two days."

As your son demonstrates an ability to choose and follow through responsibly, gradually allow him more choices: when to do a chore, how long to play a videogame, how to structure his study time, which friends fit him best, what college or trade school he would like to attend. Through this gradual process he learns how to be a responsible, autonomous person. When boys can effectively choose what they want, when they want it, and know how to ask for it, they will also have learned how to ask for consent and accept the answer given, as well as how to give their own consent.

Life Examples

Ron Thomas noticed that his teenage son had been texting on his cell phone more than usual the past couple of weeks. He decided to check in to see what was going on.

"Hey, Hunter, I see you've been texting more than usual lately. Any particular reason?"

"No, just snapchatting with a friend."

"Would this friend by any chance be a girl?"

"Yeah, a girl."

"Are you at that boyfriend-girlfriend spot?"

"Not yet, but I think it could turn out that way."

"Well, before that happens I have a couple of comments," Ron said. He then waited to get eye contact from his son. "I know we talked about this before, but it's just a quick reminder. Whenever you're together with this girl, regardless of what you're doing, make sure you ask for her opinion. If you want to hold her hand, ask her first. If you want to sit next to her at lunch, ask her if it's okay before you sit down. Get her permission, and respect whatever answer she gives you."

"I know, Dad."

"Yes, Hunter, I know that you do. I just wanted to remind you."

*****

"You have the opportunity to be with your friends," Kyle Wilson told his eleven-year-old son. "Your responsibility is to be home on time. As you know, in our family, opportunity equals responsibility.

If you honor the responsibility, there will be more opportunities to be with your friends. If you decide not to honor it, you've chosen to have less time with your friends."

Leo understood exactly what his father meant. He had heard that statement many times previously. He knew his father wasn't kidding when he talked that way.

This type of language was the cornerstone of the Wilsons' effort to have their children grow into independent, self-responsible adults. They knew that the more their children learned to handle opportunities, the more responsible they would be with choices and decisions as adults.

*****

Shane came home from graduate school to visit with his family for the Thanksgiving holiday. He was accompanied by Tonya, a young woman he'd been dating for six months. As the family got ready to sit down for dinner, Shane asked Tonya what she would like to drink with her meal. He gave her options that included several alcoholic beverages plus milk, juice, and water. Tonya replied, "I'm not sure. I'll let you decide for me."

After a brief moment of silence, Shane said, "I don't think it's appropriate for me to decide if you're going to put alcohol into your body. You decide, and I'll be glad to get you whatever you'd like."

"Okay," said Tonya, "A glass of white wine, then."

Hearing this brief interchange, Shane's parents glanced at each other and smiled. They knew what this type of dialogue represented: a relationship of mutual respect and shared consent.

*****

Cassandra received a phone call from her son's school while she was at work. She was asked to pick him up because he had been suspended for inappropriate behavior on the playground at recess. When Cassandra arrived at the school, she was given the information that her six-year-old son had kissed a girl while they were on the climbing structure. This was considered sexual harassment by the school administration, behavior which required a mandatory two-day suspension.

The drive home was quiet. Casey sat in the back seat staring at his feet. Cassandra was deep in thought as she contemplated what to say and what to do next. Her mind was filled with questions. *What should I say to him about his behavior? Did he just kiss her, or were they talking about kissing? Has he done this before with her or any other girl? Did the girl want a kiss? Did she say he could kiss her? He's only in first grade. Will he really understand consent? Are kids his age even able to give consent to one another? Is it really sexual harassment? How am I going to get him to understand the seriousness of his actions?*

When they finally reached home, Cassandra asked Casey to join her at the kitchen table to talk about what happened. As they sat down across from each other, Cassandra started the conversation by asking Casey to explain what happened. He said, "I was over by the swings with Martha. We go over there and sit and talk."

Cassandra interrupted. "Do you do that a lot, or was this the first time?"

"We do that almost every day."

"What do you talk about?"

"Mostly stuff on YouTube or TV."

"Okay, the two of you were talking, and then what happened?"

"Well, she was talking about something she saw on YouTube, and I just looked at her and I wanted to kiss her, so I did." He paused, lowered his head slightly and continued, "I didn't hurt her."

Cassandra leaned forward. "Casey, I know you didn't mean to hurt her. And it's important for you to understand that it is never okay to touch someone, even when it's gentle, if they don't want to be touched. You gave Martha a kiss, and that's a type of touch. That is not a way that first-graders touch each other, and we don't know if Martha wanted to be touched at all."

"But Mom, you give me a hug and a kiss every night before I go to sleep, and you don't ask me," Casey pointed out.

"Well, Casey, I should," his mother responded. "And I will from now on. If you don't want a hug or a kiss, you can say, 'No thanks, not tonight,' and I won't give you one." Cassandra paused and then said, "We can talk more about this later. Let's get a snack and a drink. What would you like?"

Conclusion

Asking for and giving consent is not as simple as just saying no or yes. Toxic masculinity has twisted the definition of consent and left women standing on the sidelines watching a male-dominated culture attempt to redefine it. The solution lies in teaching boys how to become autonomous while retaining responsibility. Boys need opportunities to learn how to handle life's responsibilities. Lessons are not learned the first time they are presented. Redefining consent requires many opportunities for boys to learn to make responsible choices within the experiences they encounter. Mistakes will be made along the way. See and treat those mistakes as growth opportunities for your son.

Heeding the Call for Change

The 9 lessons you have been introduced to in *Dissolving Toxic Masculinity* incorporate parenting strategies that Valerie and I have learned throughout our education, careers, and experiences with our own children. Although they are not the only lessons you will need to raise your boys to be empathic, compassionate men, they embody the techniques and strategies we have relied on the most in raising our sons.

During the process of organizing and writing the parenting material for this book, I became aware of other voices throughout the country shouting the demand for change in how we view and think about masculinity. Campaigns such as #MeToo and Time's Up have opened the door for women to come forward with allegations of sexual harassment and abuse and confront the men who have forced them to remain silent. The call for change rings loud and clear. The time for that change is now!

In preparing to write the book, I thought deeply about the changes that need to happen in order to raise boys who don't become misogynistic men. I imagined a world where sexual harassment is a problem of the past. I envisioned a planet where women and men hold positions of power in equal proportions. I imagined boys growing up in families where accountability is implemented with gentleness and love; where men use language that takes ownership of their feelings and actions; where empathy and compassion are embraced as vital components of masculinity; where cooperation rather than competition is celebrated; where men consider diversity a healthy component of a family, a workplace, and a community; where intimate relationships are built upon mutual consent and appreciation. I envisioned what the world will look like when parents raise their boys to be empathetic, compassionate, responsible men. That vision became my guide in writing the 9 lessons that comprise the book.

The world I imagined is possible. It is achieved one family at a time. The world begins to change when we change how we raise our boys. Putting into practice the lessons in *Dissolving Toxic Masculinity* can be your contribution to that change.

About the Author

Thomas B. Haller

MDiv., LMSW, ACSW, CMFSW, DST

Thomas Haller is an internationally recognized presenter, an award-winning author of nine highly acclaimed books, and a psychotherapist maintaining a 30-year private practice as a child, adolescent, and couples therapist. He is a Certified Master Forensic Social Worker, an AASECT certified diplomate of sexuality therapy, and a certified sports counselor. Thomas is also the chief parenting and relationship correspondent to WNEM TV 5 (CBS affiliate). He can be seen on television answering viewers' questions three days a week in his Family Matters segment.

Thomas is the founder and director of the Healing Minds Institute, a center devoted to teaching others to focus on and enhance the health of the mind, body, and spirit. He is president of Personal Power Press, Inc., a publishing house committed to providing parents and educators with practical material for raising responsible children.

Thomas and his partner, Valerie, maintain a not-for-profit 501 (c) (3) organization, Healing Acres, an equine retirement ranch enabling aged horses to live out their lives in a low-stress environment.

Thomas is available for workshops, seminars, student assemblies, and commencement speeches.

Website: www.thomashaller.com

Twitter: www.twitter.com/tomhaller

Facebook:

www.facebook.com/thomas.b.haller

Email: Thomas@thomashaller.com

Thomas on television answering viewer questions:

Family Matters Segment – Every Wednesday at 12:15 pm on WNEM TV5 News at Noon

Family Matters Segment – Every Sunday at 7:45 am on WNEM TV5 Weekend Wake-up

Family Matters Segment – Every Monday at 9:15 am on WNEM TV5 News at 9:00 am

Hot Topics Segment – Every Monday at 9:45 am on WNEM TV5 News at 9:00 am

Past segments can be viewed online at www.wnem.com.

Other Books and Products

www.personalpowerpress.com

THE ABRACADABRA EFFECT: The 13 Verbally Transmitted Diseases and How to Cure Them, by Chick Moorman and Thomas Haller ($19.95)

PARENT TALK ESSENTIALS: How to Talk to Kids about Divorce, Sex, Money, School and Being Responsible in Today's World, by Chick Moorman and Thomas Haller ($15.00)

THE ONLY THREE DISCIPLINE STRATEGIES YOU WILL EVER NEED: Essential Tools for Busy Parents, by Chick Moorman and Thomas Haller ($14.95)

THE TEACHER TALK ADVANTAGE: The Five Voices of Effective Teaching, by Chick Moorman and Thomas Haller ($24.95)

TEACHING THE ATTRACTION PRINCIPLE TO CHILDREN: Practical Strategies for Parents and Teachers to Help Children Manifest a Better World, by Thomas Haller and Chick Moorman ($24.95)

COUPLE TALK: How to Talk Your Way to a Great Relationship, by Chick Moorman and Thomas Haller ($24.95)

DENTAL TALK: How to Manage Children's Behavior with Effective Verbal Skills, by Thomas Haller and Chick Moorman ($24.95)

Qty.	Title	Price Each	Total
		Subtotal	
		Tax MI residents 6%	
		S/H (see chart below)	
		Total	

Please add the following shipping & handling charges:
$1 - $15.00 -- $4.95
$15.01 - $30.00 -- $5.95
$30.01 - $50.00 -- $6.95
$50.01 and up 15% of total order
Canada: 20% of total order. US funds only, please.

Ship To:

Name: _____

Address: _____

City: _____ State:_____ Zip: _____

Phone: _____

☐ **American Express** ☐ **Discover** ☐ **VISA**

☐ **MasterCard** ☐ **Check/Money Order**

(payable in US funds)

Card #_____-_____-_____-_____

Expiration Date _____/_____ CVV _____

Signature_____

PERSONAL POWER PRESS, INC.
5225 Mile Rd, Bay City, MI 48706
customerservice@personalpowerpress.com
www.personalpowerpress.com

Newsletters

Thomas Haller publishes two FREE e-mail newsletters one for parents and another for educators. To subscribe to either of them, e-mail: customerservice@personalpowerpress.com.

Or you can visit:

www.personalpowerpress.com or www.thomashaller.com